MAINE
COOK BOOK

Cooking Across America
Cookbook Collection™

**GOLDEN
WEST ☼
PUBLISHERS**

Front and back cover photos courtesy Maine Office of Tourism, Augusta (www.visitmaine.com)

Compiled by Virginia D. Clark

Acknowledgments

Maine Potato Board; Blueberry Board of Maine; Wild Blueberry Association of North America; Wild Blueberry Commission of Maine; University of Maine; Maine Lobster Promotion Council; Maine Department of Marine Resources

Cooking Downeast by Marjorie Standish (page 54)
    www.downeastbooks.com.
Kitchen With a View Cook Book (pages 34, 43, 57, 77)
    The Keeper's House: 207-367-2261
Pilgrim's Inn Cook Book (pages 8, 35, 55, 78)
    The Pilgrim's Inn: 207-348-6615
Maine Courses (pages 14, 31, 84).
    The Maine Diner: 207-646-0406
    www.mainediner.com

Printed in the United States of America

ISBN #1-885590-35-0

2nd Printing © 2003

Golden West Publishers, Inc.
4113 N. Longview Ave.
Phoenix, AZ 85014, USA

(800) 658-5830

Visit our website: goldenwestpublishers.com

Table of Contents

Introduction

Welcome to the Pine Tree State! Home to wild blueberries, savory lobsters, crisp apples, hearty potatoes and so much more! Many years ago Mainers learned to live off the land and enjoy nature's bounty. From simple beginnings have evolved these fantastic recipes which reflect Maine's culinary heritage and history.

The **Maine Cook Book** presents mouth-watering recipes utilizing native Maine foods; from family favorites to restaurant specialties and country inn delights this cookbook is sure to please everyone looking for a true taste of America's most eastern state.

Enjoy lobster, scallops, salmon, haddock and many other seafood specialties as well as wild game recipes featuring venison, grouse and even moose! And we've got fiddlehead recipes! These wild favorites are legendary in Maine, try picking some yourself or sample them from local supermarkets. Many of these recipes feature fresh farm produce; Maine has hundreds of small farms and orchards.

This unique state offers spectacular scenery, from rugged coastlines to pastoral farms and gardens. Maine is a traveler's paradise with incredible outdoor adventures, quaint shopping villages and four-season activities.

As part of our *Cooking Across America Cookbook Collection* we are happy to share these time-honored recipes with you. And we hope, if you are visiting Maine, that you take this book home with you as a keepsake and introduction to the wonderful foods of Maine!

Maine Facts

Size—19th largest state with an area of 35,387 square miles
Population—1,286,670
State Capital—Augusta
Statehood—March 15, 1820, the 23rd state admitted to the Union
State Nickname—Pine Tree State
State Song—"State Song of Maine" words
and music by Roger Vinton Snow
State Motto—*"Dirigo"*—"I direct"
State Fish—Landlocked Salmon
State Cat—Maine Coon Cat
State Insect—Honeybee
State Gemstone—Tourmaline

State Flower
Eastern White Pine Cone
and Tassel

State Animal
Moose

State Bird
Chickadee

State Tree
Eastern White
Pine

Famous Mainers

Walter Van Tilburg Clark, *writer;* **Cyrus Curtis,** *publisher;* **Dorothea Dix,** *civil rights reformer;* **Dustin Farnum,** *actor;* **John Ford,** *film director;* **Melville Fuller,** *jurist;* **Winslow Homer,** *painter;* **Henry Wadsworth Longfellow,** *poet;* **Sarah Orne Jewett,** *author;* **Stephen King,** *writer;* **Linda Lavin,** *actress;* **Hiram Stevens Maxim,** *inventor;* **Edna St. Vincent Millay,** *poet;* **Marston Morse,** *mathematician,* **Frank Munsey,** *publisher;* **Edmund S. Muskie,** *politician;* **Walter Piston,** *composer;* **George Palmer Putnam,** *publisher;* **Kenneth Roberts,** *historical author;* **Edwin Arlington Robinson,** *poet;* **Nelson A. Rockefeller,** *politician*; **Margaret Chase Smith,** *politician;* **Percy Lebaron Spencer,** *inventor;* **Francis & Freelan Stanley,** *inventors;* **Harriet Beecher Stowe,** *writer;* **John Hay Whitney,** *publisher;* **Andrew Wyeth,** *painter.*

Maine Visitors Information: 1-888-624-6345

Soups, Stews & Chowders

Kale & Red Potato Soup

"Serve this soup with thick Italian or French bread slices."

Tala Henry—Wells

1/2 stick lightly salted BUTTER
1 lg. ONION, chopped
3-4 cloves GARLIC, chopped fine
6 med. CARROTS, peeled and sliced
4 oz. MUSHROOMS, sliced
1 bunch fresh KALE, chopped into large pieces
6 cups BOILING WATER
3 cubes BEEF BOUILLON
6-8 med. RED POTATOES, parboiled,
    cut into chunks
PEPPER
DILL SEASONING
GARLIC POWDER

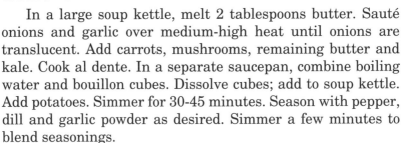

In a large soup kettle, melt 2 tablespoons butter. Sauté onions and garlic over medium-high heat until onions are translucent. Add carrots, mushrooms, remaining butter and kale. Cook al dente. In a separate saucepan, combine boiling water and bouillon cubes. Dissolve cubes; add to soup kettle. Add potatoes. Simmer for 30-45 minutes. Season with pepper, dill and garlic powder as desired. Simmer a few minutes to blend seasonings.

Serves 6-8.

Potato, Leek & Fontina Soup

"This is an ideal soup for the cool autumn months. It is the starch content of russet potatoes that gives this soup body and a smooth consistency."

Chef Terry Foster—*Pilgrim's Inn Cookbook,* Deer Isle

1 Tbsp. OLIVE OIL
3 LEEKS, white part only, finely diced
2 cloves GARLIC, minced
2 stalks GREEN ONIONS, finely diced
2 Tbsp. DRY SHERRY
2 1/2 lbs. RUSSET POTATOES, peeled and diced
5 cups CHICKEN BROTH
1 cup HEAVY CREAM or MILK
SALT and PEPPER
5 oz. FONTINA CHEESE, cut into small cubes
2 Tbsp. chopped fresh CHERVIL
2 Tbsp. chopped fresh CHIVES

In a large saucepan, heat oil over medium-high heat. Add leeks, garlic and green onions. Sauté for 4-5 minutes, stirring occasionally. Add sherry and cook for 2 minutes. Add potatoes and chicken broth. Bring to a boil. Reduce heat to a low simmer and cook for 15 minutes. Add cream, salt and pepper. Continue to cook until the potatoes are tender, about 5 minutes. Remove soup from heat and stir in cheese. Transfer soup to a blender and purée until smooth. Add seasoning as desired. Ladle soup into bowls. Serve garnished with chervil and chives.

Early to Bed, Early to Rise!

Eastport is the most eastern city in the United States. It is considered to be the first place in the United States to receive the rays of the morning sun!

Seafood Stew

*"I always serve this with crusty French garlic bread
to sop up all the sauce."*

Judith Nelson—Rockland

3 lbs. MUSSELS	3 cans (14.5 oz. ea.) DICED
1 Tbsp. OLIVE OIL	TOMATOES
1 ONION, minced	1/2 lb. SCALLOPS
3 cloves GARLIC, minced	1/2 lb. COD, cut into
3/4 tsp. THYME	bite-size pieces
3/4 tsp. OREGANO	1/2 cup PARSLEY FLAKES
1 1/2 cups DRY WHITE WINE	2 Tbsp. BUTTER
1 Tbsp. LEMON JUICE	FRENCH GARLIC BREAD

Under running water, clean mussels thoroughly, scraping off beard. In a large kettle, heat oil over medium-high heat. Add onion, garlic, thyme and oregano. Sauté about 3 minutes until onions are soft, stirring occasionally. Add wine and lemon juice. Cook for 10 minutes or until sauce has reduced to half. Add tomatoes, mix well. Add mussels. Cover and cook about 4-5 minutes or until mussels open. As they open, place them in a bowl. Discard any that do not open. Cover to keep warm. Place scallops and cod in sauce and cook for 7 minutes or until scallops are opaque. Add parsley, butter and mussels. Serve in soup bowls with French bread on the side.

Rockland

Rockland, one of Maine's major fishing ports and known as the "Lobster Capital of the World" as well as "Schooner Capital of Maine," is also the birthplace of Edna St. Vincent Millay. Ferries to nearby islands and visiting the Rockland Breakwater Light on Penobscot Bay and the Owls Head Light are favorite visitor activities. Also popular are the North Atlantic Blues Festival in July and the Annual Maine Lobster Festival in early August.

Pork & Sauerkraut Stew

*"It isn't all lobsters and seafood in Bar Harbor.
Try this for a delicious supper!"*

Martha Browne—Bar Harbor

3 cups SAUERKRAUT
3 lbs. boneless PORK BUTT
SALT and PEPPER
3 Tbsp. MARGARINE
2 cloves GARLIC, minced
1 lg. ONION, chopped
2 tsp. PAPRIKA

1 1/2 tsp. DILL WEED
1 can (14.5 oz.) CHICKEN
   BROTH
2 tsp. CORNSTARCH
1/2 cup SOUR CREAM
Chopped PARSLEY

Drain sauerkraut, rinse and drain again. Set aside. On a cutting board, cut pork into bite-size pieces. In a bowl, season pork with salt and pepper. In a 5-quart kettle, melt 2 tablespoons of margarine. Add pork and brown on all sides. Remove pork from kettle and set aside. Add more margarine to kettle if needed to make about 2 tablespoons. Sauté garlic and onion (scraping bits off bottom of pan), until onion is tender. Stir in paprika and dill weed. Return pork and juice from meat to kettle. Add sauerkraut and chicken broth. Cover. Simmer until pork is tender, a little over an hour. Skim off and discard fat. Cook rapidly, uncovered, until sauce has cooked down to about a cup of liquid. Combine cornstarch with a small amount of water and stir into stew. Add sour cream and stir until stew simmers. Spoon into serving dishes and sprinkle with parsley.

Serves 4-6.

Bar Harbor

Acadia National Park comprises most of Mount Desert Island. At the entrance of the park lies the beautiful city of Bar Harbor. Once the summer playground of wealthy and famous Americans, today's Bar Harbor is popular with travelers throughout the year. Activities include music festivals, museum tours, biking, hiking, sailing, whale watching and much more!

Maine Potato & Beef Stew

Maine Potato Board—Presque Isle

2 lbs. CHUCK BEEF, cut into 3/4-inch cubes
2 lg. ONIONS, sliced thick
2 cups HOT WATER
1 BAY LEAF
1 1/2 tsp. WORCESTERSHIRE SAUCE
1 tsp. SUGAR
SALT, PEPPER and GARLIC POWDER
4 lg. MAINE POTATOES, peeled and chunked
5 CARROTS, peeled and sliced 1/4-inch thick
5 stalks CELERY, sliced 1/4-inch thick
1/4 cup FLOUR
1/3 cup COLD WATER

In a 3-quart microwaveable dish, mix together beef, onions, hot water, bay leaf, Worcestershire sauce and sugar. Add salt, pepper and garlic powder to taste. Microwave on High for 6 minutes. Stir and rotate once. Microwave on Medium-High for 35 minutes, stirring occasionally. Add potatoes, carrots and celery. Cover and microwave on Medium-High for 35 minutes more, or until meat and vegetables are tender. Blend flour and cold water together. Stir into stew. Microwave on High for 5 minutes longer, stirring once. Remove bay leaf before serving.

Serves 6.

Presque Isle

Presque Isle sits on the edge of the "North Maine Woods," the gateway to fantastic outdoor adventure. While four-season activities abound, the long winter allows for incredible snowmobiling, cross-country and downhill skiing. Double Eagle II Park features a replica of the balloon used in the first successful transatlantic flight (1978). Just south is the 600-acre Aroostook State Park which encompasses Quaggy Jo Mountain and Echo Lake and is home to a wide variety of wildlife and birds.

Salmon Chowder

"I make this chowder for a cold winter night's supper."

Eunice Scarborough—Auburn

4 med. POTATOES,
   peeled and diced
1 3/4 cups WATER
2 cups MILK
SALT
1 pkg. (10 oz.) frozen MIXED
   VEGETABLES
1 med. ONION, chopped fine

2 Tbsp. MARGARINE
1 Tbsp. FLOUR
1 lb. SALMON FILLET, cubed
1 tsp. WORCESTERSHIRE
   SAUCE
2 tsp. LEMON JUICE
DILL

In a large saucepan, combine potatoes, water, 1/2 cup milk and salt. Bring to a boil. Lower heat and simmer until potatoes are tender. Add vegetables. Cover and remove from heat. In a saucepan, sauté onion in margarine until soft. Stir in flour. Cook for 1 minute before adding remaining milk, stirring to make a smooth sauce. Add to potato mixture. Return saucepan to heat and bring to a boil; lower heat. Add salmon, Worcestershire sauce and lemon juice. Heat thoroughly and pour chowder into soup bowls. Add a dash of dill to top of each serving.

Serves 4.

Corn Chowder

Dorothy Marple—Liberty

1 cup chopped ONION
1/2 cup chopped CELERY
2 Tbsp. MARGARINE
3 cups fresh CORN
1 1/2 cups peeled, diced
   POTATOES

1 can (14.5 oz.) CHICKEN
   BROTH
SALT and PEPPER
1/4 tsp. THYME
2 cups MILK
1 cup HALF AND HALF

In a large saucepan, sauté onion and celery in margarine until tender. Add corn, potatoes, broth and seasonings. Cook on medium-high heat for 10-15 minutes or until potatoes are done. Add milk and half and half. Heat through, stirring constantly. Pour into soup bowls and serve.

Corn & Lobster Chowder

"This is a favorite dish at York Harbor Inn!"

Exec. Chef Gerald Bonsey, CEC—York Harbor Inn, York Harbor

8 oz. finely diced ONIONS
8 oz. finely diced CELERY
2 oz. CLARIFIED BUTTER
2 lbs. fresh CORN KERNELS
1 qt. CHICKEN STOCK
8 oz. ROUX
1 lb. unpeeled RED POTATOES,
    cubed
1/2 tsp. WHITE PEPPER
1/2 Tbsp. SALT
1 BAY LEAF
1/2 tsp.THYME
1/4 cup finely diced RED
    BELL PEPPER
1/4 cup finely diced GREEN
    BELL PEPPER
1 lb. LOBSTER MEAT, cubed
3 cups HEAVY CREAM

Combine onions, celery and clarified butter in a stockpot and sauté until tender. Add corn, stir and cover. Sauté gently until corn is cooked. Add chicken stock and bring to a boil, stirring occasionally. Whisk in roux, turn off heat for 5 minutes. Turn heat to medium high and bring to a boil, stirring often. Add potatoes, spices and bell pepper; gently simmer until potatoes are cooked. Cool. When ready to serve, heat in a double boiler, add lobster meat and heavy cream.

Yield: 1 gallon.

Cream of Fiddlehead Soup

"Bob Cram, another outdoor writer and friend from Medway came up with this tasty method of sampling fiddleheads."

Bill Graves—Outdoor Columnist and Author, Presque Isle

3/4 cup chopped GREEN ONIONS
1/4 cup BUTTER
3 cups CHICKEN STOCK
1 1/2 cups peeled and cubed
    POTATOES
2 cups FIDDLEHEADS
1/2 tsp. SALT
1/4 tsp. PEPPER
1 1/2 cups MILK
Chopped CHIVES
CROUTONS

In a skillet, sauté onions in butter for five minutes. Stir in chicken stock, potatoes, fiddleheads and seasonings. Cover and simmer until potatoes are tender (about 30 minutes). Purée fiddlehead mixture in blender until smooth. Stir in milk. Serve hot or cold, garnished with chives and croutons.

Seafood Chowder

From the *Maine Courses* Cookbook—The Maine Diner, Wells

1 1/2 qts. WATER	2 cups MILK
1 1/2 lb. LOBSTER	1/4 cup PARSLEY FLAKES
1/2 lb. STEAMING CLAMS	1 Tbsp. PAPRIKA
1/2 lb. SCALLOPS	2 med. POTATOES, peeled
1/2 lb. (26-30 count) SHRIMP	and diced
1 can (10 oz.) BABY CLAMS,	4 oz. SALT PORK, finely diced
undrained	1 med. ONION, finely diced
1/4 lb. BUTTER	SALT and PEPPER
2 cups LIGHT CREAM	OYSTER CRACKERS

Bring water to a boil in a large pot. Add lobster and cook for 15 minutes with lid on. Remove lobster. Add clams to pot and cook until they open. Remove clams. Add scallops and shrimp to pot and cook until done. Do not remove. Pick lobster meat, break into bite-size pieces and add to pot. Clean tomalley out of lobster cavity and add to pot. Add baby clams with juice, butter, cream, milk, parsley and paprika. In a saucepan, boil potatoes until just tender; add to other ingredients in pot. In a skillet, sauté salt pork until brown. Add onion and cook until tender. Add salt pork and onions to pot. Simmer on low until hot. Season to taste. Pour into soup bowls and top with oyster crackers.

Smoked Haddock Chowder

Emory Sanderson—Augusta

1/4 cup BUTTER	SALT and PEPPER
1 med. ONION, diced	3 cups WATER
2 lbs. SMOKED HADDOCK	1 stalk CELERY, chopped
FILLETS, cubed	3 cups MILK
3 med. POTATOES, cubed	1/2 cup crushed OYSTER
1/8 tsp. CLOVES	CRACKERS

In a skillet, melt butter and sauté onions until translucent. Add fillets, potatoes, cloves, salt and pepper to taste, water and celery. Simmer gently until potatoes are tender. Stir in remaining ingredients and bring to a boil.

Salads & Side Dishes

Scallop Salad

"This is a good luncheon salad for a hot summer day."
Barbara Hayes-Warren—South Portland

1 cup thinly sliced CELERY
1/4 cup chopped ONION
1/2 cup GREEN SEEDLESS GRAPES, halved
1/4 cup toasted slivered ALMONDS
1 can (10 oz.) MANDARIN ORANGES, drained
1/4 cup MAYONNAISE
1/3 cup SOUR CREAM
Dash of SALT
1 lb. cooked SCALLOPS, cut into bite-size pieces
SPINACH
PAPRIKA

In a mixing bowl, combine celery, onion, grapes, almonds, oranges, mayonnaise, sour cream and salt. Fold in scallops and toss mixture gently. Arrange in spinach cups and garnish with paprika.

Maine Seafood Salad

Shirley Allerton—Augusta

2 cups bite-size CRABMEAT, LOBSTER or SHRIMP
1 cup finely diced CELERY
2 Tbsp. PICKLE RELISH
1 Tbsp. finely diced ONION
SALT and PEPPER
1/2 cup SALAD DRESSING
2 HARD-BOILED EGGS, chopped
LETTUCE
TOMATO SLICES, halved

Combine all ingredients except lettuce and tomato. Serve on a bed of lettuce and garnish with tomato slices.

How to Sound Like a "Mainah"

Drop some of these into your conversations: Ayuh (yup, sure, okay). Cah (a four wheel vehicle, not a truck). Chowdah (chowder). Crittah (any furry animal). Numb (dumb, stupid). Scrid (a tiny piece). Wicked (very, as in wicked good, wicked bad, etc.)

Smith's Farm
Broccoli Salad

Greg Smith—Smith's Farm Inc., Presque Isle

Salad:
1 bunch fresh MAINE BROCCOLI   1/4 cup RAISINS
   cut into bite-sized pieces   2 Tbsp. diced RED ONION
1 cup shredded CHEDDAR CHEESE   3 Tbsp. BACON BITS

Dressing:
3/4 cup HELLMAN'S® MAYONNAISE   1/4 cup SUGAR
2 Tbsp. VINEGAR   1/8 tsp. PAPRIKA

In a bowl, combine salad ingredients. In another bowl, combine dressing ingredients. Toss dressing with salad and serve.

Creamy Chicken Mold

"This is a great summer luncheon salad."

Rachel Allen—Waterville

2 env. (1 oz. ea.) UNFLAVORED GELATIN
2 cups COLD WATER
1 can (10.75 oz.) CREAM OF CHICKEN SOUP
1 Tbsp. LEMON JUICE
1 pkg. (3 oz.) CREAM CHEESE, softened
2 cups cooked CHICKEN, cut into bite-size pieces
1 Tbsp. chopped GREEN ONION
1/2 cup chopped CELERY
1/2 cup chopped GREEN BELL PEPPER
SALAD GREENS

In a saucepan, mix gelatin in 1 cup of water. Place over low heat. Stir until the gelatin is dissolved. Remove from heat. In a mixing bowl, combine chicken soup and lemon juice. Blend in cream cheese, gelatin and remaining cup of water. Mix well. Chill until partially set. Fold in chicken, green onion, celery and bell pepper. Pour mixture into a 5-cup decorative mold. Chill until firm. When ready to serve, unmold onto a bed of salad greens.

Lewiston & Auburn

Lewiston, the second largest city in Maine, lies on the east bank of the Androscoggin River, with Auburn, its twin city, on the west bank. In the 1850s, water power from the river was harnessed and both cities benefited greatly. Lewiston is the home of Bates College and the Thorncrag Bird Sanctuary. In the 1870s, Auburn shipped two million pairs of shoes per year. Today, the two cities are often referred to as the "industrial heart" of Maine.

Green & Red Slaw

"This makes a colorful Christmas salad."

Audrey Little—Washington

3 cups shredded GREEN CABBAGE
1/2 cup sliced GREEN ONIONS
1/4 cup chopped PARSLEY
1/2 cup chopped GREEN BELL PEPPER
1/2 cup chopped CELERY
1/2 cup chopped unpeeled GREEN APPLE
1/2 cup CIDER VINEGAR
1/3 cup SALAD OIL
3 Tbsp. SUGAR
1/8 tsp. DRY MUSTARD
SALT and PEPPER
2 cups chopped RED CABBAGE
1/4 cup chopped RED BELL PEPPER
RED and GREEN SEEDLESS GRAPES

In a large bowl, combine green cabbage, green onions, parsley, green bell pepper, celery and apple. In another bowl, make dressing by mixing vinegar, oil, sugar and seasonings. Pour all but 2 tablespoons of salad dressing over salad. Mix well and set aside. In a smaller bowl, combine red cabbage and red bell pepper. Toss with remaining dressing. Cover each bowl. Chill overnight. When ready to serve, stir each salad. Place green slaw in bottom of a glass serving bowl, add the red slaw to top. Garnish with grapes.

Maine Sardine Salad

Maine Department of Marine Resources—Augusta

2-3 cans (3.75 oz. ea.) MAINE
   SARDINES, drained
1/2 cup minced GREEN BELL
   PEPPER

1/4 cup minced ONION
1 cup diced CUCUMBER
1 cup MAYONNAISE
SALT and PEPPER

Reserve 8 sardines for garnish. Place remaining sardines in a mixing bowl and add remaining ingredients. Toss lightly and serve on a bed of **LETTUCE** with a **Dash of PAPRIKA**. Garnish each serving with 2 whole sardines on top.

Yucatan Mussel Salad

Marinating overnight brings out all the flavors
of this great salad!

The Great Eastern Mussel Farms, Inc.—Tenants Harbor

1 lb. GREAT EASTERN® MUSSELS
3 cups WATER
1/2 cup medium diced RED BELL PEPPER
1/2 cup medium diced GREEN BELL PEPPER
1/3 cup chopped CELERY
1/3 cup medium diced ONION
1/4 cup finely chopped CILANTRO
1 sm. JALAPEÑO PEPPER, finely chopped,
    veins and seeds removed
2 cups COUSCOUS, cooked
1/4 cup fresh LIME JUICE
2 Tbsp. + 2 tsp. OLIVE OIL

In a large kettle, steam mussels in water over high heat for 4-5 minutes or until shells open. Remove meat from shells. Combine with all other ingredients in a glass or ceramic bowl. Mix well, cover and refrigerate. Allow to marinate 6-12 hours.

About Maine Mussels

Cultivated mussels have thin, light jet-black shells. They range in size from 2 to 3 inches. Mussels contain more heart healthy Omega-3 fatty acids than any other shellfish.

• *If in doubt about a mussel being alive, put ice on it for 15 minutes, then tap the shell gently. If the mussel does not move and the shell gaps, discard it!* • *Discard any mussels that have cracked shells or that do not open after steaming.* • *Do not store mussels in airtight containers or plastic bags—they need to breathe.* • *Wash mussels well under cold running water.* • *Remove beards with a stiff brush.*

Fried Potato & Clam Cakes

*"I fry these in peanut oil because it makes the cakes
nice and brown."*

Charlotte Barnes—Bar Harbor

2 cups peeled, grated
   POTATOES
1 sm. ONION, grated
1 clove GARLIC, minced
1 can (6.5 oz.) MINCED CLAMS,
   liquid reserved

1 EGG, beaten
1 Tbsp. melted BUTTER
1/2 tsp. BAKING POWDER
1 Tbsp. FLOUR
SALT and PEPPER
OIL for frying

Squeeze all excess moisture from the potatoes and onions after grating. In a mixing bowl, add potatoes, onion, garlic, clams, egg and butter. Mix well. In a small bowl, mix baking powder, flour and seasoning. Add to potato mixture. The batter should be the consistency of whipped cream. Thin with clam liquid if necessary. Add oil to a hot griddle and drop batter from a teaspoon onto it. Brown on both sides and serve.

Maine Potato Salad

Maine Potato Board—Presque Isle

5 med. MAINE POTATOES
GARLIC POWDER
1 med. ONION, chopped
1/2 cup chopped CUCUMBER
1/2 cup chopped GREEN BELL PEPPER
1/2 cup chopped RED BELL PEPPER
2 Tbsp. chopped fresh PARSLEY or 2 tsp. dried
SALT and PEPPER
FAT FREE FRENCH DRESSING
1/2 cup FAT FREE MAYONNAISE

In a saucepan, boil potatoes, peeled or unpeeled, until tender. Slice or dice potatoes; sprinkle sparingly with garlic powder. In a salad bowl, combine potatoes, vegetables, parsley and salt and pepper to taste. Pour in enough French dressing to coat salad lightly. Toss. Cover and chill for 8 hours or overnight. Just before serving, add mayonnaise and toss gently.

Baked Stuffed Potatoes

"These are good for that extra-special dinner."

Charlotte Barnes—Bar Harbor

6 lg. BAKING POTATOES	1 cup fresh MUSHROOMS,
3 Tbsp. MARGARINE	chopped
1/4 cup MILK	SALT and PEPPER
1 HARD-BOILED EGG, chopped	1 cup grated SWISS CHEESE

Scrub potatoes well, then bake for 50-60 minutes in a 375° oven or until they test done. Remove from oven. Slice tops off and scoop out pulp without breaking shell. Combine pulp with margarine, milk, egg, mushrooms, seasonings and half of the cheese. Fill shells and sprinkle with remaining cheese. Bake for 10-15 minutes or until thoroughly heated and tops have browned.

About Maine Potatoes

Of the 117 varieties of potatoes grown in Maine, the two most well-known are the Green Mountain and Katahdin. Green Mountain, the most flavorful and easiest to grow, originated in Vermont, hence the name. This species is the one that made Maine potatoes famous. It is good for frying, baking and mashing as it has a high starch quality.

The other well-known Maine potato, Katahdin, has a low starch quality with a thin skin and a waxy texture. It is best suited for soups, salads and boiling.

Potato & Onion Bake

"These go very well with roast leg of lamb."

Bernice Tompkins—Augusta

2 lbs. RED POTATOES
2 Tbsp. VEGETABLE OIL
4 Tbsp. BUTTER
2 lg. SWEET SPANISH ONIONS, thinly sliced
SALT and PEPPER
2 cans (14.5 oz. ea.) BEEF BROTH

In a saucepan, boil potatoes for 10 minutes. Drain. Peel and slice to 1/4-inch thick. In a skillet, heat oil with 2 tablespoons butter. Sauté onions until limp and not quite brown. Remove skillet from heat. Butter a 13 x 9 baking dish. Starting and ending with potatoes, alternately layer potatoes and onions in baking dish. Season. Add just enough beef broth to cover. Dot with remaining butter. Bake in a 350° oven for 1 hour or until potatoes are tender and all liquid absorbed. Add more broth if necessary during cooking.

Grilled Corn & Potato Salad

"The grilled corn gives this salad a smoky flavor."

Theda Lyden—Harraseeket Inn, Freeport

2 lbs. RED POTATOES
2 ears CORN
3 stalks CELERY, diced

1/2 sm. RED ONION, diced
1/2 cup MAYONNAISE

Place quartered potatoes in a saucepan, cover with water and cook until tender. Drain and cool. Remove husks from corn and grill until done. Cut kernels off cobs. Cool. Toss all ingredients together when serving.

Serves 8-10.

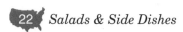

Fiddlehead Quiche

"This popular Maine delicacy can only be found in the late spring when the ferns (an ostrich fern) are very young and still have their tightly coiled heads that resemble the curled end of a violin—hence their name. Pick fiddleheads when 2- to 6-inches high, snapping off the tops with only an inch of stem attached. Clean by tossing them in the air to blow off brown casings, or, wash in several water baths in a colander."

Bill Graves—Outdoor Columnist and Author, Presque Isle

1 sm. TOMATO	1 cup chopped FIDDLEHEADS
4 Tbsp. BUTTER	3 lg. EGGS
2/3 cup diced ONION	1/2 cup CREAM
1 (9-inch) unbaked PIE SHELL	1/2 cup MILK
8 oz. finely diced SWISS	1/2 tsp. OREGANO
CHEESE	2 tsp. chopped PARSLEY
1 1/2 Tbsp. FLOUR	

Preheat oven to 400°. Remove skin and seeds from tomato; chop, cover and refrigerate for 30 minutes. In a skillet, melt butter and sauté onion until soft; spread over bottom of pie shell. In a bowl, combine cheese with flour and then spread mixture over onion. Cover cheese with fiddleheads. In a small bowl, beat eggs; combine with remaining ingredients and pour over fiddleheads, Bake 35 minutes or until tests done.

Fiddlehead Puff

Bill Graves—Outdoor Columnist and Author, Presque Isle

1 cup BISQUICK	1 lb. fresh FIDDLEHEADS
1/4 tsp. SALT	1 cup shredded CHEDDAR
1 cup MILK	CHEESE
2 EGGS, beaten	

Grease a 1 1/2 quart casserole dish. In a bowl, combine Bisquick, salt, milk and eggs; blend until smooth. Stir in fiddleheads and cheese. Pour mixture into casserole dish and bake at 350° for 55-60 minutes or until tests done.

Acorn Squash Stuffed with Cranberries

"I make this delicious dish with fresh squash from my garden. It goes great with turkey or chicken."

Audrey Little—Washington

2 ACORN SQUASH
1/2 cup fresh CRANBERRIES
1/2 cup chopped NUTS
1/2 tsp. CINNAMON

2 Tbsp. melted MARGARINE
1/2 cup packed BROWN SUGAR

Cut squash in half lengthwise. Remove seeds. In a mixing bowl, combine remaining ingredients. Fill squash halves with cranberry mixture. Bake in a 350° oven for 50 minutes or until squash is tender.

Saco

This sister city of Biddeford was settled in 1631 and incorporated as Pepperellboro in 1762. The city was renamed Saco in 1805. Water power from the Saco River made an ironworks industry possible in the early days of Saco. Today, commerce plays a leading role in the economy.

Cranberry Relish

Cornforth House is a historical home built in the early 19th century. Some rooms still have the original fireplaces.

Cornforth House Restaurant—Saco

1/2 cup RED WINE VINEGAR
1 cup RASPBERRY VINEGAR
1 cup grated ORANGE PEEL
1 qt. whole fresh CRANBERRIES

1 1/4 cups WHITE WINE
1/2 cup HONEY
1 Tbsp. ORANGE JUICE

In a large pot, combine vinegars and orange peel. Cook until reduced to 1/3 liquid. Add remaining ingredients. Cook until fruit is soft. Remove cranberries. Cook remaining liquid until it becomes syrupy. Add fruit. Mix well. Chill.

Maine Lobster Recipes

Truly the Ultimate White Meat!

Harvested from cold coastal waters, Maine lobster has a distinctive flavor that is both mild and slightly sweet. It makes an impressive entrée, delicious served in pasta dishes, salads, quiches, bisques, soups, stews and sandwiches. Lobsters are low in fat, calories and cholesterol and high in nutrition. They can be baked, broiled, boiled, grilled, microwaved, sautéed or steamed.

Live lobsters should be active and their tails should curl under them. Black marks or holes in the shell are not caused by contamination, but rather from the result of wear and tear, or indicate an older lobster that has not recently shed its shell.

They are most commonly greenish brown/black, but can also be blue, yellow, red or white. All except the white ones turn red when cooked.

Hard shell versus new shell: New shell lobsters have recently molted (shed) in order to grow and the lobster has not yet grown into its new shell. Lobsters increase in size about 20% every time they molt. New shell lobster lovers claim the meat is sweeter while hard shell lobster lovers feel theirs has more meat. Actually, the lobster in the shell of a new shell lobster is not smaller, it just hasn't grown into its new shell.

(Courtesy of the Maine Lobster Promotion Council)

How to Cook Maine Lobster

The two most common ways to cook whole lobsters are steaming and boiling.

Steaming lobster

Pour 2 inches of seawater (or salted water—add 2 tablespoons of salt for each quart of water) into a pot large enough to comfortably hold the lobsters. Some cooks also place a steaming rack large enough to hold the lobsters above the water, in the bottom. Bring water to a rolling boil over high heat. Place lobsters in the pot, cover tightly, return to a boil as quickly as possible and start counting the time.

Steam a lobster for 13 minutes per pound, for the first pound. Add 3 minutes per pound for each additional pound thereafter. For example, a 2-pound lobster should steam for 16 minutes and a 1 1/2-pound lobster should steam for 14 1/2 minutes.

Boiling lobster

The number of lobsters to be boiled determines the minimum kettle size. The water should fill the pot one-half to not more than two-thirds full. Bring salted water to a rolling boil over high heat. Place lobsters head first into the pot, completely submerging them.

Cover the pot tightly and return to a boil as quickly as possible. When water boils begin counting the time. Regulate the heat to prevent water from boiling over, but be sure to keep the liquid boiling throughout the cooking time.

Boil a lobster for 10 minutes per pound, for the first pound. Add 3 minutes per pound for each additional pound thereafter. For example, a 2-pound lobster should boil for 13 minutes and a 1 1/2-pound lobster should boil for 11 1/2 minutes.

Note: These times are for hard shell lobsters; if cooking new shell lobsters, reduce boiling or steaming time by three minutes. When the antennae pull out easily, the lobsters are done.

How to Buy Maine Lobster

Thanks to scientific advances, Maine lobster meat is now available all year long. Maine lobster meat can be purchased fresh, frozen or pasteurized (seasonally).

LIVE: Quality live lobsters should be active with their tails curled tightly and their claws not hanging limply. Live lobsters are most commonly greenish brown/black, but can also be blue, yellow, red or white.

WHOLE COOKED (Frozen): Fully cooked then frozen. Available whole or split in half. Thaw and heat according to package instructions.

WHOLE BLANCHED (Frozen): Partially cooked (blanched), then frozen. Blanching prevents the meat from sticking to the shell. Produces a product similar to uncooked and should be prepared according to any favorite recipe.

MEAT: Lobster meat, fully cooked, available fresh or frozen, includes the meat from claws, knuckles, tail and body of lobster.

TAILS: Frozen in the shell, this is the largest part of the lobster. Available whole or split. Tail sizes range from 3-6 ounces. Great for grilling, broiling and baking.

COCKTAIL CLAW: Claw intact, fully cooked. Shell has been scored for ease in cracking when served. No tools required.

LOBSTER FILLETS: Whole, uncooked lobster tails, frozen with shell removed. Excellent for any recipe calling for lobster meat. (Seasonal)

CLAW and KNUCKLE MEAT: Fully cooked. Includes meat from the claws and knuckles of the Maine lobster. This meat can be used in salads, sandwiches, stews or any favorite lobster dish.

MEDALLIONS: Prepared from frozen uncooked lobster tails, produced by cutting the tail into sections with the shell still attached. Ideal for preparation where presence of the shell may be aesthetically desirable. (Seasonal)

How to Eat Maine Lobster

Twist off large claws. Crack each claw with a nutcracker, pliers, knife or rock. Separate the tail from the body and break off tail flippers. Insert a fork and push the tail meat out in one piece. Remove and discard the black vein which runs the entire length of the tail meat as well as the tomalley. Open the body by cracking it apart sideways. Lobster meat lies in the four pockets, or joints, where the small walking legs are attached. The small walking legs also contain excellent meat which can be removed by sucking on the ends of the legs.

Tomalley [TOM-al-ee or toh-MAL-ee]

Considered a delicacy, tomalley is the green-colored liver of a lobster. It may be eaten alone but is often also added to sauces.

Lobster au Gratin

"This is a perfect dish to prepare ahead and pop in the oven just before guests arrive. It also travels well."

Maine Lobster Promotion Council Recipe—Bangor

3 cups MAINE LOBSTER MEAT
3 cups CRABMEAT or HADDOCK
3 cups LIGHT CREAM
6 EGG YOLKS
3 Tbsp. RICE
6 Tbsp. BUTTER
3 Tbsp. FLOUR
3 Tbsp. SHERRY
SALT and PEPPER
BREAD CRUMBS for topping

Mix all ingredients, except bread crumbs. Pour into a buttered casserole dish. Sprinkle with bread crumbs and dot with butter. Bake in a 400° oven for 15-30 minutes.

Serves 12.

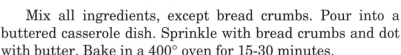

The "Great Taste of Maine Lobster Governor's Tasting and Culinary Competition"

This prestigious event is sponsored by the Maine Lobster Promotion Council. It is held at the Blaine House (Governor's Mansion) in Augusta.

Cabbage & Lobster Soup

"Spruce Point Inn has received the Governor's Award in multiple categories and most recently, the Silver Medal awarded to Chef William Hynes in 2001."

Susan Clough—Spruce Point Inn, Boothbay Harbor

2 Tbsp. SWEET BUTTER
1/2 cup peeled and thinly sliced ONION
1/3 cup peeled, diced to 1/4-inch CARROTS
1 (1 lb.) CABBAGE
LOBSTER STOCK (see next page)
SALT and freshly ground PEPPER
2 Tbsp. minced CHIVES
2 Tbsp. DANDELION TOPS
LOBSTER MEAT (see next page)

In a large pot, melt butter over medium-high heat. Add onion and carrots. Sweat for 3-4 minutes, stirring often. With a sharp knife, core and remove thick veins of cabbage and discard. Cut leaves into 1/2-inch pieces. Add cabbage to pot. Sweat vegetables for 3 minutes more. Pour **Lobster Stock** over vegetables. Add seasoning to taste. Cook until cabbage is soft, 20-30 minutes. Keep warm until ready to serve. Just before serving, add lobster meat to the soup. Mix well.

Serves 4.

(Continued on next page)

Cabbage & Lobster Soup (continued)

Lobster Stock

1 LEEK, split and coarsely chopped
1 CARROT, peeled and thickly sliced
1 stalk CELERY, thickly sliced
1 BAY LEAF
1 clove GARLIC
2 (1 lb. ea.) LOBSTERS
1 cup fresh SWEET CORN

In a large pot, bring 3 quarts of water to a boil. Add leek, carrot, celery, bay leaf and garlic. Boil 10 minutes. Rinse lobsters under cold water. Add to pot. Cover with a lid and boil for 4 minutes. Remove lobsters and set aside to cool. Keep lobster stock warm. When lobsters have cooled, twist off the 8 hind claws from each lobster body and add to stock. Extract meat from shells, slice into 1/2-inch pieces and refrigerate. Rinse shell pieces under cold water; add to stock. Bring stock to a boil and boil for 15 minutes. Strain stock, discarding shells and vegetables. Add corn to stock and set aside.

Casco Bay Lobster Stew

"This stew is even better when re-heated the next day."
Chef Wilfred Beriau (www.lovemainelobsters.com)—S. Portland

3 LOBSTERS
2 Tbsp. BUTTER
1/4 cup diced ONION
1-2 BAY LEAVES
 CRACKED PEPPER

2 qts. LIGHT CREAM
TABASCO®
1/4 cup SHERRY
Chopped HERBS of choice

Cook lobsters; crack (reserve juices), remove meat and dice. In a soup pot, add butter, onion, bay leaf and pepper; sauté until onion is tender. Add lobster juice and reduce slightly. Stir in cream, lobster meat and Tabasco and heat slowly to develop the flavor. When ready to eat, add sherry and serve, sprinkled with chopped herbs of your choice.

Serves 6.

Maine Lobster Quesadillas

"This recipe was a Second Place Winner in the 1996 'Cooking with Maine Lobster' Consumer Recipe Contest."

Barbara J. Desso—St. Albans

2 (8-inch) FLOUR TORTILLAS
3 oz. LOW FAT JACK, CHEDDAR or MOZZARELLA
    CHEESE, shredded
1 cup chopped LOBSTER MEAT
2-3 slices ONION
3 slices TOMATO, cut in half
Thin slivers of GREEN BELL PEPPER
SALT and PEPPER

Spray a skillet with cooking spray. Over medium-high heat lay a tortilla in pan. When slightly warm, spread half of cheese over tortilla. Spread lobster meat, onion, tomato and bell pepper over cheese. Add remaining cheese to top. Add seasoning. Place remaining tortilla on top and press gently. Cook until bottom of tortilla starts to brown and cheese begins to melt, about 2 minutes. Turn, cook one minute more. Cut into wedges and serve.

Maine, SOLD for $6,000!

In 1677, Massachusetts bought Maine from the English Gorges family for $6,000. A movement for separation from Massachusetts which began in 1785, finally resulted in an affirmative vote in 1819. Maine became a state in 1820.

Lobster Stew

From the *Maine Courses* Cookbook—The Maine Diner, Wells

1 1/4 lbs. LOBSTER, boiled
1 qt. HALF AND HALF
1 cup MILK
1/4 lb. BUTTER

1/2 tsp. TOMALLEY (liver)
SALT and PEPPER
OYSTER CRACKERS
PAPRIKA

Cut lobster meat into bite-size pieces. Reserve tomalley. In a saucepan, combine half and half, milk, butter, tomalley, salt and pepper. Bring to a simmer over low heat; add lobster. Ladle stew into bowls, add crackers and sprinkle with paprika.

Lobster & Wild Mushrooms

*"This recipe serves two people. I arrange angel hair pasta on
a plate and nest the lobster and sauce in the middle."*

Chef Wilfred Beriau (www.lovemainelobsters.com)—S. Portland

1 Tbsp. BUTTER	3-4 Tbsp. HEAVY CREAM
1/2 tsp. minced SHALLOTS	DRY SHERRY
6 SHITAKE MUSHROOMS,	SALT and PEPPER
sliced, stems removed	1 Tbsp. fresh BASIL, sliced
2-3 Tbsp. WHITE WINE	8 oz. LOBSTER MEAT, cut into
1/2 tsp. LEMON JUICE	large chunks

In a skillet, melt butter and sauté shallots for one minute
without browning. Add mushrooms and cook until tender.
When mushrooms are cooked, add wine and lemon juice and
reduce by one half. Add cream, sherry, seasonings and lobster
and cook gently until just bubbly, about 3 minutes.

Lobster-Stuffed Potato

"This is an old Maine recipe that I use on a regular basis"

Chef Wilfred Beriau (www.lovemainelobsters.com)—S. Portland

6 BAKING POTATOES, baked, scooped (shells reserved)
3/4 cup diced CELERY
1/2 cup diced ONION
1 cup SCALLOPS, medium diced
1 Tbsp. BUTTER
SALT and PEPPER
24 oz. LOBSTER MEAT, steamed, diced
3/4 cup shredded CRAB MEAT
3/4 cup SHRIMP
1/2 cup SCALLIONS, sliced
SHERRY
1 cup MAYONNAISE or SOUR CREAM

Preheat oven to 350°. In a skillet, sauté celery, onion and
scallops in butter until slightly cooked. Season with salt and
pepper, then add remaining ingredients (including potato pulp);
toss gently. Divide mixture evenly among potato shells, top
with **FRESH BREAD CRUMBS** and bake until heated throughout.

Lobster Bisque

"Our restaurant, overlooking the beautiful Boothbay Harbor, was built into the side of an original 1917 tugboat named 'The Maine'. Steam powered, she worked the Maine coast for years."

Chef Michael Ham—Tugboat Inn, Boothbay Harbor

3 (1 1/4 lbs. ea.) fresh MAINE LOBSTERS
8 oz. LOBSTER BUTTER (see below)
2 oz. SHERRY
Dash of CAYENNE
4 oz. FLOUR
12 oz. HEAVY CREAM
16 oz. MILK

In a large pot, boil lobsters for 12-15 minutes. Cool lobsters and then remove meat from tails, claws and knuckles. Reserve lobster shells. In a large saucepan, simmer lobster meat with **Lobster Butter** and sherry for 5 minutes. Add cayenne and flour. Mix well and cook for 5 minutes. Add cream and milk. Simmer until smooth and creamy.

Lobster Butter

LOBSTER SHELLS   **1 lb. BUTTER**   **8 oz. WATER**

In a medium saucepan, simmer lobster shells in butter and water for 30 minutes. Strain through fine strainer.

Boothbay Harbor

Boothbay Harbor is a picturesque seaport with an old New England ambiance. Over the years, the region's strong shipbuilding and fishing heritage has slowly transitioned to a resort and vacation theme. Featured activities now include river and ocean cruises as well as whale watching, sailing and deep-sea fishing.

Lobster with Pasta

"Our guests often request this dish!"

Judith Burke—The Keeper's House, Isle au Haut

2 Tbsp. OLIVE OIL
2 cloves GARLIC, minced
MEAT from 2 steamed LOBSTERS,
   cut into chunks
2 Tbsp. DARK RUM
JUICE of 1 LEMON
JUICE of 1 LIME

4 GREEN ONIONS, chopped
1 tsp. fresh DILL
1 tsp. fresh TARRAGON
1/2 tsp. PEPPER
1/2 cup HEAVY CREAM
Cooked PASTA

In a large skillet, heat oil and brown garlic over high heat. Add lobster meat. Cook for 1 minute. Stir in all ingredients except cream and pasta; reduce heat. Stir in cream and heat gently. Serve over pasta.

Isle au Haut

The town of Isle au Haut is on an island by the same name just off the coast of Maine. Portions of the island are part of Acadia National Park. The island can be reached via ferry from Stonington.

Lobster Casserole

1 lb. LOBSTER MEAT
3 Tbsp. BUTTER
3 Tbsp. FLOUR
3/4 tsp. DRY MUSTARD
SALT and PEPPER
2 cups RICH MILK (part cream)

3 slices WHITE BREAD,
   crusts removed
3 Tbsp. SHERRY
1/2 cup BUTTERED
   BREAD CRUMBS

Cut lobster into bite-size pieces. Melt butter in a skillet; add lobster and cook until meat turns slightly pink. Combine flour with seasonings and sprinkle over lobster; add milk slowly, stirring to blend. Cook, stirring gently, until mixture thickens. Tear bread into pieces and stir into skillet; add sherry. Pour all into a greased casserole dish. Top with bread crumbs and bake for 30 minutes at 350° or until top is golden brown.

Lobster Gazpacho

"Please note that it is essential to use fresh, ripe tomatoes in this recipe, as they provide a foundation of flavor for the soup."

Chef Terry Foster—*Pilgrim's Inn Cookbook,* Deer Isle

4 TOMATOES, peeled, seeded and diced
1 CUCUMBER, peeled, seeded and diced
1 RED BELL PEPPER, diced
1 sm. ONION, diced
1 sm. CELERIAC, peeled and diced
1 stalk CELERY, diced
1 clove GARLIC, minced
2 Tbsp. chopped fresh CHERVIL
1 Tbsp. chopped fresh PARSLEY
2 Tbsp. chopped fresh CILANTRO
3 Tbsp. OLIVE OIL
1 Tbsp. LIME JUICE
Few drops TABASCO®
2 cups TOMATO JUICE
SALT and PEPPER
2 cups LOBSTER STOCK
LOBSTER MEAT
2 AVOCADOS, peeled and diced for garnish
FRESH CHIVES, chopped for garnish

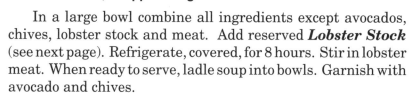

In a large bowl combine all ingredients except avocados, chives, lobster stock and meat. Add reserved **Lobster Stock** (see next page). Refrigerate, covered, for 8 hours. Stir in lobster meat. When ready to serve, ladle soup into bowls. Garnish with avocado and chives.

(Continued on next page)

Deer Isle

Deer Isle is reachable by automobile over a high narrow suspension bridge. The island is a cluster of quiet communities where fishing is the mainstay of the economy. The beautiful scenery, quiet woods and open fields have been a popular draw for artists and craftspeople for more than a century.

Lobster Gazpacho (continued)

Lobster Stock

2 (1 1/2 lbs. ea.) LOBSTERS	1 Tbsp. chopped fresh THYME
2 Tbsp. OLIVE OIL	1 Tbsp. chopped fresh
1 sm. ONION, diced	CHERVIL
1 CARROT, diced	1 BAY LEAF
1 stalk CELERY, diced	1 cup DRY WHITE WINE
1 clove GARLIC, peeled	6 cups WATER
2 Tbsp. chopped fresh PARSLEY	1 tsp. LEMON JUICE

In a large pot, steam lobsters for 10 minutes. Remove from heat and cool. Remove lobster meat from tail and claws. Reserve shells. Dice meat and set aside for gazpacho. Split body of lobster in half. Discard green tomalley, sand sac behind eyes and gill tissues. Rinse body section under cold water. Chop body, tail and claw shells into small pieces for the stock.

In a large stock pot, heat olive oil over medium-high heat. Add onion, carrot, celery and garlic. Sauté for 3-4 minutes, stirring occasionally. Add lobster shells and remaining stock ingredients. Bring to a boil. Reduce heat and simmer slowly for 30 minutes. Strain stock through cheesecloth or fine strainer. Reserve 2 cups of stock for gazpacho. Chill until needed.

Lobster Puffs

Maine Lobster Promotion Council Recipe—Bangor

2 cups FLOUR	1 cup MILK
1/2 tsp. SALT	1/2 lb. MAINE LOBSTER
Several dashes of CAYENNE	MEAT, chopped
3 tsp. BAKING POWDER	2 cups PEANUT OIL
1 EGG, well-beaten	

In a mixing bowl, sift together flour, salt, cayenne and baking powder. In another bowl, blend together egg and milk. Stir in lobster meat. Add to flour mixture and mix well. In a skillet, heat peanut oil until hot but not smoking. Carefully drop lobster mixture by rounded tablespoons into hot oil. Fry for 3 minutes or until golden. Allow plenty of room in pan for puffs to cook. Drain on paper towels.

Potato Crisp with Lobster, Spinach & Gruyère

"This recipe was a winner in the "Great Taste of Maine Lobster Governor's Tasting and Culinary Competition."

Susan Clough—Spruce Point Inn, Boothbay Harbor

2 (1 lb. ea.) LOBSTERS
1 cup fresh SPINACH
2 Tbsp. chopped GREEN ONIONS
1 cup WHITE WINE
JUICE of 4 lg. LEMONS
1 cup CREAM
1 qt. SHORTENING or OIL for frying
2 POTATOES, peeled
1/2 cup shredded GRUYÈRE CHEESE

Cook lobsters in boiling water for 8 minutes. When cooked, remove meat from tails and claws. Set aside for later use. Cook spinach and set aside. Preheat oven to 350°. Using a 1-quart pot, sauté onions until translucent. Add white wine and lemon juice. Reduce heat to 1/3. Add cream. Reduce heat to 1/2. Sauce is done. Reserve. Heat shortening to 375°. Shred potatoes through a box grater. Using 2 (2-oz.) ladles, place half of potato inside one ladle. Cover it with other ladle. Cook in hot shortening until crisp. Make second potato crisp. Place cooked spinach in potato crisp. Add lobster meat. Top with Gruyère cheese. Add sauce. Place in a preheated oven until cheese melts or about 3 minutes. Serve hot with **Pesto** as a garnish.

Serves 2.

Pesto

1 bunch fresh BASIL
2 Tbsp. imported PARMESAN
   CHEESE

1 clove GARLIC
1/2 cup OLIVE OIL
1/4 cup PINE NUTS

Place all ingredients in a food processor and blend.

Lobster Lasagna

"If you do not have pasta sheets, use lasagna noodles."
Heidi Duffett, Head Chef—Arundel Wharf Restaurant,
Kennebunkport

3 lbs. RICOTTA CHEESE
3 EGGS
2 Tbsp. GARLIC OIL, divided
1 Tbsp. fresh PARSLEY, chopped
2 cups grated ROMANO CHEESE
4 cups HEAVY CREAM
4 PASTA SHEETS or 12 LASAGNA NOODLES
1 lb. SPINACH, stemmed
2 lbs. LOBSTER MEAT, chopped into bite-size pieces
2 cups shredded PARMESAN CHEESE
3 cups shredded CHEDDAR CHEESE

In a bowl, mix ricotta cheese, eggs, 1 tablespoon garlic oil and parsley; set aside. In a saucepan, over medium-high heat, simmer Romano cheese, cream and remaining garlic oil until mixture thickens to sauce consistency; set aside. Spread a thin layer of Romano sauce in the bottom of a 13 x 9 baking pan. Cover with pasta sheet. Spread 1/2 of ricotta mixture on pasta sheet. On top of ricotta mixture, spread 1/2 of the spinach. Cover with pasta sheet. Spread 1/2 of lobster meat over pasta sheet. Pour small amount of ricotta mixture over lobster. Add remaining spinach and cover with pasta sheet. Add remaining lobster meat. Cover with ricotta mixture. Place the final pasta sheet over all and spread Parmesan, then cheddar over sheet. Bake at 350° for 25-30 minutes. Top servings with remaining Romano cheese sauce.

Kennebunkport

Kennebunkport is home to many galleries and museums. The Seashore Trolly Museum houses one of the world's oldest and largest collections of electric trolley cars. Near this popular coastal city there is a unique waterspout caused by the incoming tide blowing through rock formations at Cape Arundel.

ck Book ★ ★ ★ ★

Lobster Newburg

"This is a great dish to serve guests and to use up leftover lobster meat."

Andrea Swonburg—Portland

2 Tbsp. BUTTER	2 cups EVAPORATED MILK
1 Tbsp. minced PARSLEY	1/2 cup WATER
1 Tbsp. finely chopped CELERY	SALT and PEPPER
1 Tbsp. finely chopped ONION	2 cups LOBSTER MEAT,
1 Tbsp. finely chopped GREEN	chunked
BELL PEPPER	2 EGG YOLKS
1 cup sliced MUSHROOMS	1/4 cup SHERRY
2 Tbsp. FLOUR	6 PATTY SHELLS

In a saucepan, melt butter. Add parsley, celery, onion, bell pepper and mushrooms. Cover and cook gently for 10 minutes, stirring occasionally. Blend in flour. In a bowl, combine evaporated milk with water; measure 2 cups and add to saucepan. Cook, stirring frequently, until mixture is thick and smooth. Season to taste. Add lobster meat. In a small bowl, beat egg yolks and remaining milk together. Add egg mixture and sherry to creamed lobster. Cook for 1 minute. Serve at once in freshly baked patty shells.

Portland

Once the capital of Maine and currently the largest city in the state, this city has exhibited an indomitable will to survive. Following three nearly disastrous events; Indian attack, British attack and then, in 1866 a horrendous fire, Portland was reconstructed in the classic Victorian style which is still represented today, particularly in the six-block area known as Old Port. Viewing the "Whaling Wall", a 950-foot mural depicting sea life at the Maine State Pier; cruising around the 365 Calendar Islands in Casco Bay; hiking in the 76-acre Fore River Sanctuary, or visiting Henry Wadsworth Longfellow's childhood home are only a few of the activities that make this city a favorite destination.

Maine Lobster Recipes 39

Lobster Stuffed Chicken with Boursin Cheese Sauce

"This is York Harbor Inn's signature dish!"

Exec. Chef Gerald Bonsey, CEC—York Harbor Inn, York Harbor

Cracker Stuffing:
   2 oz. finely diced ONIONS
   2 oz. finely diced CELERY
   1 oz. CLARIFIED BUTTER
   1 oz. DRY SHERRY
   1/2 Tbsp. minced GARLIC
   1/2 Tbsp. WORCESTERSHIRE SAUCE
   10 oz. crushed RITZ® CRACKERS
   1 Tbsp. sliced GREEN ONIONS
   1 Tbsp. chopped PARSLEY
   1 tsp. SALT
   1 tsp. WHITE PEPPER

8 (6 oz. ea.) boneless, skinless CHICKEN BREASTS,
   lightly pounded
1 lb. LOBSTER MEAT, medium diced

To prepare cracker stuffing: Sauté onion and celery in clarified butter until limp. Combine with remaining stuffing ingredients. Stuff each chicken breast with 2 ounces of cracker stuffing and 2 ounces of lobster meat. Bake chicken in a 350° oven for approximately 18 minutes. Top with ***Boursin Cheese Sauce*** when serving.

Boursin Cheese Sauce

2 cups HEAVY CREAM
10 oz. BOURSIN CHEESE with GARLIC and HERB

Bring cream to a boil in a 2-quart saucepan Whisk in Boursin cheese and reduce heat to very low. Cook sauce very gently, scraping the bottom of the pan with a rubber spatula often, so that the cheese does not burn. Continue cooking until sauce is lightly thickened. Sauce may be held for a short time in a warm water bath.

Serves 8.

Maine Dishes

Sole Stuffed with Crabmeat & Brie

Heidi Duffett, Head Chef—Arundel Wharf Restaurant, Kennebunkport

8 oz. BRIE CHEESE
1 lb. MAINE CRABMEAT
1 1/2 cups ITALIAN BREAD CRUMBS
1 Tbsp. chopped fresh PARSLEY
1 lb. fresh SOLE FILLETS
SALT and PEPPER
Dash of LEMON JUICE

1 tsp. WATER
2 cups HEAVY CREAM
1/2 cup grated ROMANO CHEESE
1 Tbsp. chopped GARLIC IN OIL
1 tsp. HERBS de PROVENCE
LEMON WEDGES
Sprigs of PARSLEY

Remove skin from brie and soften to room temperature. In a medium bowl, combine brie, crabmeat, bread crumbs and parsley. Mix well. On a flat surface, place fillets skin-side up. Spread 1 1/2 to 2 tablespoons of brie mixture on each. Roll up fillets and place in a baking dish. Season with salt and pepper. Add lemon juice and water to baking pan. Bake for 8-10 minutes in a 350° oven. In a saucepan, combine heavy cream, romano cheese, garlic and herbs. Simmer over medium-high heat until reduced about a third and slightly thickened. Place a couple of teaspoons of sauce on each serving plate, then place fillets on sauce. Garnish with lemon wedges and parsley.

Downeast Clambake

The quantity and type of seafood or fish used in this recipe depends on availability and personal tastes. Appetizers could include smoked trout, bluefish, salmon or tuna patés and a basket full of crackers.

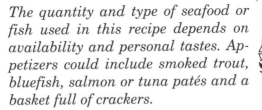

In a large enamel kettle, place a layer of **SEAWEED**. Place live **LOBSTERS (1 1/2 lb. ea. per guest)** on top of seaweed. Cover lobsters with another layer of seaweed. Add a layer of **CORN (in husks)** and another layer of seaweed. Add a layer of **ONIONS**. Add a layer of unpeeled **RED POTATOES**, more seaweed and then a layer of **STEAMER CLAMS** and/or **SHRIMP**. Add **HERBS** as desired. Cover kettle tightly and place over a fairly brisk fire. Cook for about 1 1/2 hours. Test for doneness. Serve with **LEMON WEDGES** and plenty of **MELTED BUTTER**.

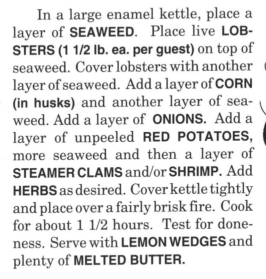

Beef Goulash

"I call this my 'Saturday Night Special.'"

Shirley Clarke—Portland

1/2 cup VEGETABLE OIL	1 med. ONION, thinly sliced
1/4 cup FLOUR	1/4 lb. MUSHROOMS, sliced
SALT and PEPPER	3/4 cup thick SOUR CREAM
2 lbs. ROUND STEAK, cut into	2 Tbsp. minced PARSLEY
bite-size pieces	1 Tbsp. PAPRIKA
2 cups BOILING WATER	Cooked NOODLES
1 sm. clove GARLIC, minced	

Heat oil in a large skillet. On a small platter, mix flour, salt and pepper with a fork. Roll beef pieces in flour to coat. Place beef in hot oil and brown on all sides. Add boiling water and garlic. Cover and simmer for 1 1/2 hours or until meat is tender. Uncover. Add onion and mushrooms. Cook to reduce some of the liquid. Add sour cream, parsley and paprika. Heat to boiling. Simmer for 10 minutes. Serve over hot noodles.

Serves 6-8.

About the Size of it!

 Maine is 320 miles long and 210 miles wide totaling in area 33,215 square miles. This includes 2,203 square miles of water.

Haddock, Sour Cream & Dill

Judith Burke—The Keeper's House, Isle au Haut

1/4 tsp. THYME	1/4 tsp. PEPPER
1 Tbsp. DILL WEED	1 cup SOUR CREAM
or 1 tsp. DRIED DILL	2 lbs. fresh HADDOCK
1/2 tsp. SUGAR	PAPRIKA
1/4 tsp. SALT	

In a small bowl, mix together all ingredients except haddock and paprika. Arrange haddock in a buttered casserole dish. Pour sour cream mixture over fish. Sprinkle with paprika. Bake at 375° for 25 minutes or until fish flakes with a fork.

Apple Stuffed Pork Chops

"This recipe can be either baked in the oven or cooked in the microwave."

Alice Alpie—Washington

8 PORK CHOPS	1/3 cup RAISINS
2 Tbsp. MARGARINE	SALT and PEPPER
1 lg. ONION, chopped	2 cups SEASONED CROUTONS
2 cups chopped APPLE	SAGE

In a skillet, sear chops in margarine. Remove from skillet and set aside. Add onions to skillet and sauté. Stir in apples, raisins, salt and pepper. Heat until warmed. Stir in croutons and sage. Arrange 4 chops on the bottom of an oven-proof dish. Place half of stuffing on top. Cover with remaining chops and top with balance of stuffing. Bake, covered, in a 350° oven for 1 hour. If using a microwave, assemble chops and stuffing in a glass casserole dish as per above. Cover with plastic wrap. Microwave on Medium-High (70°) for 14-18 minutes or until chops are thoroughly cooked. Let stand 5 minutes in microwave before serving.

Maine's First Industry

Shipbuilding became the first industry in Maine. The first ship built by English colonists in America was launched on the Kennebec River in 1607.

Clam Casserole

Rita Hanson—Washington

1 can (10 oz.) BABY CLAMS, chopped	1 can (10.75 oz.) CREAM OF MUSHROOM SOUP
2 EGGS, beaten	Dash of PEPPER
1 cup MILK	30 CRACKERS, crushed
BUTTER	

In a bowl, mix all ingredients in order given. Pour mixture into a 1 1/2-quart casserole dish. Bake at 350° for 1 hour.

Turkey & Stuffing Bake

"If you have leftover stuffing from a turkey dinner, use that instead of the stuffing mix. Just add a little water to moisten."

Natalie Crowley—Washington

3 1/2 cups STUFFING MIX
1/4 lb. MARGARINE
1 1/4 cups BOILING WATER
1 pkg. (8 oz.) frozen PEAS, CARROTS or MIXED VEGETABLES
1 can (10.75 oz.) CREAM OF CELERY SOUP
3/4 cup MILK
1 1/2 cups cooked, cubed TURKEY
FRENCH FRIED ONIONS

In a mixing bowl, combine the stuffing mix with margarine and boiling water. Blend well. In a saucepan, cook vegetables according to package directions. Drain. Add celery soup, milk and turkey to vegetables. Press stuffing mixture onto the sides and bottom of a baking dish. Pour turkey mixture in shell. Cover and bake in a 350° oven for 30 minutes. Remove from oven. Top with French fried onions. Bake, uncovered, for 5 minutes more.

Salmon Quiche

Andrea Swonburg—Portland

1/2 lb. cooked SALMON, flaked
1/2 can (7 oz.) MUSHROOMS, drained
8 oz. MONTEREY JACK CHEESE, shredded
1 (9-inch) unbaked PIE SHELL
3 EGGS, beaten
1 1/2 cups MILK

Preheat oven to 375°. In a bowl, mix salmon, mushrooms and cheese together. Spread over bottom of pie shell. In another bowl, mix eggs and milk together. Gently pour egg mixture over salmon mixture. Bake in center of oven for about 40 minutes or until quiche is golden brown and a knife inserted into center comes out clean. Cool on rack for 10 minutes before serving.

Saturday Night Supper Baked Beans

"In the early days, Bean Hole Suppers were very popular. In those years, beans were cooked by placing them in Dutch ovens which were buried in the ground surrounded by hot rocks. This contemporary recipe is for the baked beans my church serves. Saturday is the favorite day for baked bean suppers in Maine."

Annette Guttormsen—Calais

4 qts. NAVY BEANS	2 cups BROWN SUGAR
1 lb. SALT PORK	4 Tbsp. SALT
4 lg. ONIONS	1 1/2 Tbsp. DRY MUSTARD
2 cups SORGHUM MOLASSES	

Pick over beans and wash thoroughly. Place in inset pan of electric roaster. Cover with cold water and soak overnight. Simmer in the same water with control set at 300°. Cover roaster. Cook until skins pierce easily. Do not boil. Score salt pork down to rind; bury into beans. Peel and score tops of onions; bury into beans. In a bowl, combine molasses, brown sugar, salt and mustard. Pour over beans. Stir until well-mixed. Lower temperature to 250° and cook 4-5 hours, adding more water if necessary. Keep at 150° for serving.

Serves 50.

What's in a Name?

Thanks in part to its Native American heritage, Maine has some colorful (though hard to pronounce) lake names.

Try: Damariscotta, Wassookeag, Mattamiscontis, Matta-wamkeag, Meddybemps, Messalonskee, Millinocket, Mooselookmeguntic, Munsungan, Musquacook, Nah-makanta, Parmachenee, Pemadumcook, Seboomook, Umbagog, Wesserrunsett and Pocomoonshine!

Spanish Chops

"This is a good casserole to make for a winter's dinner."

Marjorie Hancock—Brunswick

1/3 cup VEGETABLE OIL
4 PORK CHOPS
1 lg. ONION, chopped
1 GREEN BELL PEPPER, chopped
1 clove GARLIC, minced
1 cup uncooked WHITE RICE
1/4 lb. MUSHROOMS, chopped
1 can (14.5 oz.) DICED TOMATOES
1 can (14.5 oz.) BEEF BROTH
1 Tbsp. CHILI POWDER
SALT and PEPPER

In a hot skillet, add oil and brown pork chops on both sides. Remove chops and place in a casserole dish. In the same skillet, sauté onion, bell pepper and garlic until slightly browned. Add rice and sauté until golden. Add mushrooms, tomatoes, broth and seasonings. Simmer for a few minutes to blend. Pour over chops. Cover. Bake in a 350° oven for 45 minutes. Remove cover. Bake for 15 minutes more.

Serves 4.

Brunswick

Originally a settlement named Pejepscot, Brunswick is an educational, industrial and recreational center, with the distinction of having the widest street in New England—Maine Street is 198 feet wide! Bowdoin College, established here in 1794, includes in its alumni; Nathaniel Hawthorne, Henry Wadsworth Longfellow, Robert Peary and President Franklin Pierce. Harriet Beecher Stowe's inspiration for "Uncle Tom's Cabin" is said to have come from a sermon given at the First Parish Church on Maine Street.

Pork Medallions
with Curry Maple Glaze

"This dish is one of our most popular menu items. For presentation we fan the medallions on the plate and garnish with the lime wedges. The glaze has a marvelous aroma and is tangy, yet sweet. We hope you enjoy it as much as our guests do."

Carolann Ouellette—Moose Point Tavern, Jackman

2 (10 oz. ea.) PORK TENDERLOINS,   **3 Tbsp. MILK**
   cut into 1 1/4-inch medallions   **1 Tbsp. FLOUR**
1/2 cup CHICKEN STOCK   **LIME WEDGES**

Add medallions to ***Maple Syrup Marinade*** and turn to coat. Marinate for at least 1 hour (or up to 3 hours). Coat a large skillet with cooking spray and heat. Add medallions, reserving marinade. Cook over moderately-high heat, turning once, until browned and cooked through, about 3 minutes per side. Transfer to a plate and keep warm. In the skillet add chicken stock and reserved marinade. Cook over moderately-high heat, scraping up any browned bits. In a bowl, gradually stir milk into flour until smooth; add to skillet. Cook, stirring until thickened, about 2 minutes. Strain sauce and serve with medallions. Garnish with lime wedges.

Serves 4.

Maple Syrup Marinade

2 tsp. CURRY POWDER   **2 Tbsp. MAPLE SYRUP**
2 Tsp. WORCESTERSHIRE   **1 clove GARLIC, minced**
   SAUCE

In a small skillet, stir curry powder over high heat until fragrant, about 2 minutes. Transfer to a shallow bowl and stir in Worcestershire, syrup and garlic.

Did You Know?

Maine boasts of 6,000 lakes and ponds, 32,000 miles of rivers and streams, 17 million acres of forestland, 3,478 miles of coastline and 2,000 islands!

Chicken Tetrazzine

"This recipe can be used with cooked turkey as well."

Rachel Allen—Waterville

1 Tbsp. OLIVE OIL
1/2 lb. fresh MUSHROOMS, sliced
1 sm. ONION, chopped
2 Tbsp. NON-FAT DRY MILK
1 1/2 Tbsp. CORNSTARCH
2 tsp. INSTANT CHICKEN BROTH
SALT and PEPPER
Pinch of NUTMEG
2 cups COLD WATER
3 cups cooked NOODLES
   (6 oz. uncooked noodles)
3 cups cooked, cubed CHICKEN BREASTS
2 Tbsp. ROMANO CHEESE
PAPRIKA

Heat oil in a skillet; add mushrooms and onion and sauté until just tender. In a saucepan, combine dry milk, cornstarch, chicken broth, seasonings and water. Mix well. Cook over medium-high heat until mixture bubbles and thickens. Arrange noodles on the bottom of a 2-quart baking pan. Spread mushrooms and onions on top. Layer with chicken. Pour sauce over all. Sprinkle top with cheese and then paprika. Bake in a 350° oven for 30 minutes.

Serves 4.

Waterville

Situated on the Kennebec River, Waterville is an industrial city and cultural center. The Abenaki Indian Tribe once held their tribal councils at nearby Ticonic Falls. Great Pond, a lake just west of Waterville, inspired the play and movie "On Golden Pond." In fact, the mailboat that was used in that production still makes its daily run.

Maine Crab-Stuffed Portobellos

"Try this delicious combination served with fresh greens."
Chef Christian Gordon—Federal Jack's Restaurant & Brew Pub,
Kennebunkport

8 PORTOBELLO MUSHROOM CAPS
OLIVE OIL
1 lb. MAINE CRABMEAT
2 EGGS, beaten
1 cup MAYONNAISE
2 Tbsp. DIJON-TYPE MUSTARD
2 Tbsp. OLD BAY® SEASONING
1 finely diced RED BELL PEPPER
1 bunch GREEN ONIONS, chopped
6 cups BREAD CRUMBS
1 lb. MESCLIN MIX (baby field greens)

Preheat oven to 350°. Brush portobello caps with olive oil. Place on a baking sheet. Bake for 5-8 minutes or until soft. In a bowl, mix crabmeat with all its juices, eggs, mayonnaise, mustard, Old Bay, 2/3 of red bell pepper and 2/3 of chopped green onions to form a paste. Slowly add bread crumbs, mixing with a wooden spoon. Stuff each portobello with crab mixture. Bake portobellos for 10-12 minutes, until warm in center. Arrange mesclin mix on serving plates, add stuffed mushrooms and drizzle tops with *Old Bay Aïoli.* Garnish with remaining red pepper and green onions.

Old Bay Aïoli

1 cup MAYONNAISE
2 Tbsp. OLD BAY® SEASONING
SALT and PEPPER

1 Tbsp. LIME JUICE
3 Tbsp. HEAVY CREAM

In a bowl, mix all ingredients together. Set aside.

Goin' Down East to Maine?

From Boston and other parts, sailing vessels sailed down-wind with the prevailing westerly wind to Maine, creating the local term, "Goin' down to Maine" or Down East.

Clam Whiffle

*"This is a quick, easy lunch for friends who
drop by unexpectedly."*

Fran Wilson—Jefferson

12 CRISPY CRACKERS	1 Tbsp. chopped GREEN BELL
1 cup MILK	PEPPER
1/4 cup BUTTER	2 tsp. minced ONION
1 can (6.5 oz.) MINCED CLAMS	Dash SALT and PEPPER
1/4 tsp. WORCESTERSHIRE	2 EGGS, beaten

In a mixing bowl, soak crackers in milk. Add remaining
ingredients in order given. Pour mixture into a 1 1/2-quart
casserole dish. Bake at 350° for 40 minutes.

Augusta

*This city succeeded Portland as the capital of
Maine in 1827. Among its earliest settlers were
John Alden and Capt. Miles Standish about whom
Henry Wadsworth Longfellow wrote in "The Court-
ship of Miles Standish." Augusta is the seat of many of
Maine's government agencies and offices.*

Haddock Burgers

"These are a big hit with my grandchildren!"

Shirley Clarke—Portland

1 lb. cooked, flaked HADDOCK	1/2 cup MAYONNAISE
1 EGG, slightly beaten	1/2 tsp. ROSEMARY
1 tsp. LEMON JUICE	1 Tbsp. grated PARMESAN
1/2 cup BREAD CRUMBS	CHEESE
1 sm. ONION, chopped	Dash of PEPPER
2 Tbsp. PARSLEY FLAKES	

In a large bowl, combine all ingredients. Mix well and then
form into 4 firm patties. In a skillet, add **OIL** and brown patties
on both sides. Serve on **HAMBURGER BUNS** with **LETTUCE** and
PICKLE or **RELISH**.

Haddock Florentine

"Our goal is to serve good quality food at a fair price with service to match, if not excel."

Erin Carey & Joseph Zdanowicz—Frogwater Cafe, Camden

2 lg. POTATOES
SALT and PEPPER
3-4 ROMA TOMATOES, sliced
1/2 cup grated PARMESAN
   CHEESE

2 bunches fresh SPINACH,
   stemmed and chopped
2 cups HEAVY CREAM
1 1/2-2 lbs. fresh HADDOCK
   FILLETS

In a saucepan, boil whole potatoes until tender. Slice. Line a casserole dish with potatoes. Sprinkle with a little salt and pepper. Layer tomatoes over potatoes. Sprinkle with Parmesan cheese and top with spinach. Pour 1 1/2 cups of cream over layered ingredients. Top with haddock fillets. Add remaining cream; salt and pepper to taste over all. Bake in a 375° oven for 25-35 minutes or until fish flakes and sauce is thickened.

Serves 4.

Camden

Camden is a charming seaside town that attracts visitors all year round. Annual events here include the National Toboggan Championships in February, Windjammer Weekend on Labor Day weekend and the Fall Festival in October.

Pan-Fried Trout

"My customers prefer this method of frying trout."

Carolann Ouellette—Moose Point Tavern, Jackman

1/4 stick BUTTER
1 TROUT, split or filleted

1/2 cup CORNMEAL
SALT and PEPPER

In a 12-inch skillet, melt butter over medium-high heat. Dredge trout in cornmeal. Raise heat to high. Season trout on both sides and place in skillet. Cook on both sides until nicely browned and interior turns white.

Baked Scallops

"I love seafood and this is so easy to prepare I make it often."

Kenneth McQuire—Bar Harbor

1 cup BREAD CRUMBS	2 Tbsp. WATER
1/2 tsp. SALT	1 1/2 lbs. SCALLOPS
Dash of PEPPER and CAYENNE	4 Tbsp. melted BUTTER
1 EGG	

In a mixing bowl, combine bread crumbs and seasonings. In another bowl, beat egg and water together. Dip each scallop in crumbs, then egg mixture, then crumbs again. Place in a baking dish. Let stand for 30 minutes. Pour melted butter over scallops. Bake in a 450° oven for 25-30 minutes or until brown and crispy. Serve with tartar sauce on the side.

Grilled Halibut Kabobs

"I serve these kabobs with a tossed green salad."

Shirley Clarke—Portland

1 lb. HALIBUT FILLETS, cut into bite-size chunks
12 ORANGE WEDGES
12 med. fresh MUSHROOMS
12 chunks CUCUMBER

Add halibut pieces to **Orange Marinade.** Marinate for at least 1 hour, stirring occasionally. When ready to cook, oil grill and heat. Arrange fish, orange wedges, mushrooms and cucumber chunks on 4 skewers. Place skewers on grill. Turn and brush with marinade several times. Grill for 8-10 minutes, or until fish is done.

Orange Marinade

1/4 cup EXTRA-VIRGIN OLIVE OIL	1/4 tsp. THYME
1/4 cup chopped ONION	1/3 cup ORANGE JUICE
1/4 tsp. ROSEMARY	1 tsp. grated ORANGE PEEL

In a bowl, combine all ingredients thoroughly.

Sautéed Halibut Steaks

"I think spinach and halibut go so well together! My grand-mother gave me this recipe when I was first married."

Barbara Hayes-Warren—South Portland

SALT and PEPPER	1 clove GARLIC, minced
2 HALIBUT STEAKS	1 Tbsp. LEMON JUICE
FLOUR	1 tsp. chopped fresh THYME
2 Tbsp. BUTTER	3 med. MUSHROOMS, sliced
2 cups chopped, cooked SPINACH	

Season steaks and dust with flour. Melt butter in a skillet and sauté steaks until done. Arrange spinach on a heated platter. Place steaks on top. Keep warm. In the same skillet, simmer garlic, lemon juice, thyme and mushrooms until mushrooms are slightly cooked. Pour over steaks and serve.

Freeport

Known as the "Birthplace of Maine," it was here that Maine was granted separation from Massachusetts and finally statehood in 1820. It is also home to the world famous L. L. Bean Company.

Escalloped Crabmeat & Oysters

From *Cooking Down East* by Marjorie Standish, courtesy of downeastbooks.com

2/3 cup BUTTER	1 2/3 cups fresh CRABMEAT
1/3 cup FLOUR	1 pt. OYSTERS, cleaned
SALT and PEPPER to taste	1 1/3 cups fine BREAD
1 pt. MILK	CRUMBS

In a saucepan, melt 1/3 cup butter and stir in flour. Cook, stirring, until well-blended. Add salt, pepper and milk. Cook and stir until thickened. In a skillet, brown bread crumbs in remaining 1/3 cup butter. Grease a casserole dish and arrange layers of white sauce, crabmeat, oysters and bread crumbs. Bake at 350° for 30 minutes.

Grilled Halibut with
Lemon-Basil Vinaigrette

"We have found that halibut from the East Coast is far superior to western halibut. This cold-water species has a faintly sweet, delicate flavor. Other firm white-fleshed fish such as grouper, turbot, cod or haddock would also work well in this dish."

Chef Terry Foster—*Pilgrim's Inn Cookbook,* Deer Isle

6 (6 oz.) HALIBUT FILLETS
1/4 cup OLIVE OIL
SALT and PEPPER
Fresh BASIL LEAVES for garnish

Prepare charcoal grill. Lightly coat halibut fillets with olive oil. Season to taste with salt and pepper. Grill fillets until firm, about 3-4 minutes per side. Place fillets on serving plates. Spoon ***Basil Vinaigrette*** over tops; garnish with basil leaves.

Basil Vinaigrette

1 tsp. DIJON-TYPE MUSTARD
3 Tbsp. LEMON JUICE
3 Tbsp. chopped fresh BASIL
1 Tbsp. chopped fresh PARSLEY
1 Tbsp. CAPERS

1 clove GARLIC, minced
1/2 cup OLIVE OIL
1 TOMATO, peeled, seeded
  and chopped
SALT and PEPPER

In a food processor, place mustard, lemon juice, basil, parsley, capers and garlic. Process for 30 seconds. With processor running, slowly pour in olive oil and process for 1 minute. Pour mixture into a serving bowl, stir in tomato. Season with salt and pepper to taste. Set aside.

The State Flower—a Pine Cone?

Most states have flowers and many states have flowers that bloom on trees as state flowers, but, Maine adopted the Eastern white pine tree's pine cone and tassel as its state flower on February 1, 1895! It was not until 1945 that the white pine itself was adopted as Maine's official state tree.

Baked Halibut in Sour Cream

"This is my favorite way to prepare fresh halibut."

Dorothy Ramshuck—Bangor

4 tsp. BUTTER, divided
2 lbs. HALIBUT FILLETS
1 tsp. SALT
1/2 tsp. TABASCO®
1 Tbsp. PAPRIKA
1/4 cup grated PARMESAN CHEESE
1 cup SOUR CREAM
1/4 cup fine BREAD CRUMBS
LEMON WEDGES
PARSLEY SPRIGS for garnish

Grease a 2-quart baking pan with 1 teaspoon of butter. Arrange fillets in pan. In a bowl, blend Tabasco, paprika and cheese with sour cream. Spread over fillets. Top with bread crumbs and remaining butter. Bake in a 350° oven, uncovered, for 30 minutes or until fish flakes easily with a fork. Serve with lemon wedges, garnish with parsley sprigs.

Calais [CAL-us]

Calais is at the mouth of the St. Croix River which forms the border between Canada and the U.S. Calais is the only international city in Maine. It is connected to St. Stephen, New Brunswick by the International Bridge. Calais is the fifth busiest port of entry into the United States on the Canadian border, with more some two million cars passing through each year. The two cities recognize their friendship with the International Festival which runs from the first Saturday to the second Sunday in August.

Scallops with Cheese Sauce

Judith Burke—The Keeper's House, Isle au Haut

1 Tbsp. OIL
2 cups finely chopped ONIONS
1 RED BELL PEPPER, chopped fine
3 lbs. SCALLOPS, cut into small pieces
BUTTER
8-10 sheets PHYLLO DOUGH
PARMESAN CHEESE
SESAME SEEDS

Add oil to a skillet and sauté onions and bell pepper on medium-high heat. Add scallops and cook for 1 minute on each side. Butter a cookie sheet. Place 2 sheets of phyllo dough on butter and brush more butter on top. Add a layer of scallop mixture, then a layer of *Cheese Sauce.* Sprinkle with Parmesan cheese. Top with 2 more phyllo dough sheets, brush with butter. Add another layer of scallops and sauce. Sprinkle more Parmesan cheese on top. Repeat until all scallops and sauce are used up. Top with 2 sheets of phyllo dough and spread with butter. Sprinkle with Parmesan cheese and sesame seeds. Bake in 350° oven for 20-25 minutes.

Cheese Sauce

2 EGGS
1 cup SOUR CREAM
1/2 cup PLAIN YOGURT
1/3 cup shredded CHEDDAR CHEESE
1/3 cup shredded PEPPER JACK
    CHEESE
1/4 cup LEMON JUICE
1 tsp. TARRAGON
1/2 tsp. DILL
1 tsp. BASIL
1/2 tsp. PEPPER

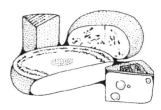

In a bowl, beat eggs. Stir in sour cream, yogurt, cheeses, lemon juice and seasonings.

Mussels Marinière

"Eat mussels as you would clams, dousing them in the sauce."

Shirley Newman—South Portland

2 lg. ONIONS, diced	Crushed PEPPERCORNS
2 cloves GARLIC, mashed	Chopped PARSLEY
2 stalks CELERY, chopped	1 cup WHITE WINE
6 Tbsp. WATER	1 tsp. LEMON JUICE
2 qts. MUSSELS	3 Tbsp. BUTTER
1 tsp. SALT	

In a heavy pot or Dutch oven, simmer onions, garlic and celery in water until tender and lightly browned. Lay mussels on top. Sprinkle with salt, peppercorns and parsley. Add wine. Cover and simmer until shells open. Lift out mussels to a serving platter. Cover with a folded napkin to keep warm. Add lemon juice and butter to sauce. Reduce sauce by about a third, boiling briskly. Strain. Pour sauce into individual serving bowls and serve with mussels.

Great Eastern's Steamed Mussels

The Great Eastern Mussel Farms, Inc.—Tenants Harbor

1/4 cup chopped GREEN ONIONS
2 cloves GARLIC, finely chopped
1/4 cup medium-diced GREEN BELL PEPPER
3-4 med. PLUM TOMATOES, medium-diced
2 tsp. OLIVE OIL
2 lbs. fresh GREAT EASTERN® MUSSELS
1/4 cup WHITE WINE
LEMON PEEL
Chopped PARSLEY

In a saucepan, sauté onions, garlic, bell pepper and tomatoes in oil for 1 minute. Add mussels and wine. Cover and cook for 4-5 minutes or until shells open. Ladle into soup bowls and garnish with lemon peel and parsley.

Bear Liver with Onions

"Do not overcook the liver, it will make it tough!"

Sonny & Dottie Gibson—North Camps, Oquossoc

1 lg. ONION, sliced
2 tsp. BACON DRIPPINGS
GARLIC POWDER
SALT and PEPPER
1 lb. BEAR LIVER, 1/2-inch thick slices

In a cast iron skillet, sauté onion in bacon drippings until tender. Set aside. Add more drippings as needed. Season liver with garlic, salt and pepper. Add to skillet. Cook on one side for 3-4 minutes. Turn and cover with cooked onions. Cook for an additional 3-4 minutes.

Oquossoc

Oquossoc is on the northwest shores of Rangley Lake. It is located in a woodland paradise with pine, spruce and fir forests where bears, bobcats, coyotes, deer and moose dwell.

Moose Swiss Steak

"I use tomato juice for more flavor, but water or beef broth works fine, too."

Madelyn Cussak—Lewiston

3 lbs. (2-inch thick) MOOSE
   STEAKS
3/4 cup FLOUR
1 tsp. DRY MUSTARD
1 1/2 tsp. SALT
1/4 tsp. PEPPER
1/3 cup VEGETABLE OIL
2 cups diced ONION
1 cup TOMATO JUICE

Wipe steaks with a damp cloth. Sift together flour and seasonings. With a mallet, beat flour mixture into steaks until all is absorbed. Heat oil in a skillet, add steaks and brown on both sides. Place steaks in a casserole dish and sprinkle with onion. Stir tomato juice into skillet juices. Pour juice over all. Bake in a 325° oven until done.

Pan Seared Venison Steaks with Red Wine Onion Sauce

Carolann Ouellette—Moose Point Tavern, Jackman

4 (8 oz.) VENISON STEAKS
PEPPER
1 Tbsp. VEGETABLE OIL

SALT and PEPPER
1 Tbsp. minced PARSLEY

Sprinkle both sides of steaks with pepper. In a large skillet, heat oil over high heat. When it begins to smoke, add 2 steaks. Sear them for 2 minutes on each side and then transfer to a heatproof plate. Repeat for remaining steaks. Season steaks with salt and pepper. Spread **Red Wine Onion Sauce** on warm plates, top with steaks. Garnish with parsley and serve.

Red Wine Onion Sauce

3 Tbsp. UNSALTED BUTTER
1/2 med. RED ONION,
**   sliced 1-inch thick**
1/2 cup DRY RED WINE

1 cup + 1 Tbsp. BEEF STOCK
HONEY
1 tsp. ARROWROOT

In a skillet, add butter and then onion. Cook onion over high heat, stirring until browned, about 2-3 minutes. Add wine and 1 cup of stock. Boil over moderately-high heat, about 4 minutes, or until liquid is reduced to 1/2 cup. Stir in a touch of honey. Dissolve arrowroot in remaining 1 tablespoon of stock; stir into sauce. Remove pan from heat.

Jackman's Moose River Bow Trip

The Moose River Bow Trip is one of the most outsanding canoe trips in Maine. The 34-mile trip begins at nearby Attean Pond and returns there via the Moose River. Much of the trip winds through Public Reserved Lands. Moose, loons, bald eagles and foxes may be viewed along the way.

Roast Grouse

"The dressing increases tenderness and juiciness of the bird."

Madelyn Cussak—Lewiston

1 (1.5 lb.) GROUSE or QUAIL	1 EGG, beaten
1/3 cup chopped CABBAGE	EVAPORATED MILK
1/3 cup chopped ONION	OLIVE OIL
1/3 cup chopped MUSHROOMS	FLOUR
1/3 cup chopped GREEN APPLE	3 slices BACON

In a mixing bowl, combine cabbage, onion, mushrooms, apple and egg. Mix well. Add enough evaporated milk to make a moist dressing. Stuff bird. Rub oil liberally over all of the exterior. Dredge in flour. Place grouse, breast up, in a shallow roasting pan. Drape with bacon slices. Roast in a 350° oven for 1 hour or until tender. Remove bacon about 15 minutes before bird is done.

Moose Roast

"This recipe is good with venison as well as moose."

Sonny & Dottie Gibson—North Camps, Oquossoc

1 (4-5 lb.) MOOSE ROAST
1 sm. ONION, cut into small wedges
1 med. APPLE, peeled, cored and cut into wedges
COOKING OIL
GARLIC POWDER, SALT and PEPPER to taste
4-5 slices BACON

With a paring knife, make 3 to 4 rows of slits in roast. Put small wedges of onion and apple into each slit. Rub outside of roast with cooking oil. Season with garlic powder, salt and pepper. Wrap slices of bacon around roast every 3 inches. Secure with toothpicks. Place roast in pan and add about 1 inch of water to bottom. Cover pan with foil. Cook at 350° for 30 minutes per pound. Remove foil for last 15 minutes. Moose should be cooked medium to well.

Baked Salmon Fillet

"I use this recipe for halibut, haddock and cod,
but prefer it with salmon."

Kenneth McQuire—Bar Harbor

1 SALMON FILLET	1/4 cup chopped PARSLEY
SALT and PEPPER	1/2 cup sliced MUSHROOMS
OLIVE OIL	1 clove GARLIC, minced
1 stalk CELERY, chopped	4 ROMA TOMATOES,
1 med. ONION, chopped	chopped
1/2 cup chopped GREEN BELL	1 can (8 oz.) TOMATO SAUCE
PEPPER	1/2 cup RED WINE

Wash and dry salmon. Season with salt and pepper and rub with olive oil. Place salmon in a baking dish. In a bowl, combine celery, onion, bell pepper, parsley, mushrooms, garlic and tomatoes. Spread over salmon. Bake in a 350° oven for 15 minutes. In a bowl, mix tomato sauce and wine together. Spread over salmon. Bake another 45 minutes or until salmon flakes easily with a fork.

Roasted Trout
with Herb Rub

Carolann Ouellette—Moose Point Tavern, Jackman

Herb Rub:
   1 tsp. minced TARRAGON
   1 Tbsp. minced fresh PARSLEY
   1 tsp. GARLIC
   2 Tbsp. OLIVE OIL
   1 Tbsp. LEMON JUICE
   SALT and PEPPER

1 (3/4 lb.) TROUT
LEMON WEDGES

Preheat oven to 450°. In a bowl, thoroughly combine rub ingredients. Spread rub on both sides of trout. Place trout in a baking pan and roast, without turning, for 15 minutes. Flesh should flake easily with a fork. Serve with lemon wedges.

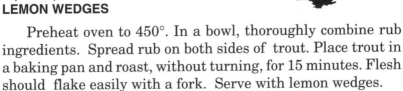

Venison Chops or Steaks

"This is one of the favorites in North Camps' dining room"

Sonny & Dottie Gibson—North Camps, Oquossoc

1 med. ONION, sliced
2 cloves GARLIC, chopped
BACON DRIPPINGS or MARGARINE
2 med. APPLES, peeled and sliced
4 VENISON CHOPS or STEAKS

In a 12-inch cast iron skillet, sauté onion and garlic in bacon drippings. When tender, add apples. When apples begin to get tender, move to one side of pan. Add more bacon drippings. Add chops. Cover with onion and apple mixture. Cook 3-4 minutes per side or until done, turning once.

Maine's Natural Assets

Maine is rich in natural assets—542,629 acres of state and national parks, including the 92-mile Allagash Wilderness Waterway, Acadia National Park (second most visited national park in the U.S.) and Baxter State Park (location of Mt. Katahdin and the end of the Appalachian Trail).

Broiled Salmon

Evelyn Novotny—Bangor

1/2 cup BUTTER, melted
SALT
1/8 tsp. DILL
6 (1 1/2-inch thick) ATLANTIC SALMON STEAKS
LEMON JUICE

In a cup, combine butter, salt and dill. Brush over steaks and then sprinkle with lemon juice. Arrange steaks on a lightly greased broiler rack. Broil 6-inches from heat about 5 minutes per side or until fish flakes easily with a fork. Serve on a bed of **SPINACH** surrounded with **TOMATO WEDGES, STUFFED OLIVES, chopped GREEN ONIONS** and sprinkle a **dash of LEMON JUICE** over the top.

Fried Fish

"Try this for your game fish such as salmon, brook trout (also known as square tail), perch and chub."

Larry LeRoy—Medawisla Wilderness Camps, Greenville

3 (8 to 10-inch) PERCH	Pinch of SALT
WATER	Pinch of PEPPER
1/3 cup MAYONNAISE	2 cups dry INSTANT
2 Tbsp. LEMON JUICE	MASHED POTATOES

In a saucepan, boil fish in water until meat falls off bones. Reserving broth, place meat in a small mixing bowl. Add mayonnaise, lemon juice, salt and pepper. Mix well. Add potatoes and enough leftover broth to form a batter, similar to that of pancakes. Create pancake size cakes in a hot cast iron skillet; brown on both sides.

Greenville

Greenville, the gateway to the great North Woods, lies at the south end of Moosehead Lake, the largest lake in Maine. It is a center for both winter and summer outdoor activities.

Codfish & Rice

Shirley Allerton—Augusta

4 strips BACON	Dash of CELERY SALT
2 HARD-BOILED EGGS	Cooked RICE
2 1/2 cups cooked COD, flaked	Parsley
1/4 tsp. PAPRIKA	LEMON WEDGES

In a skillet, cook bacon until crisp. Remove and set aside to drain on paper towels. Separate egg yolks and whites into two bowls; dice. Add fish, paprika and celery salt to egg whites and mix. Crumble bacon and return to skillet; add fish mixture. Stir frequently until heated through. Divide rice between serving plates and top with fish mixture. Garnish with egg yolks, parsley and lemon wedges.

Serves 4-6.

New England Boiled Dinner

The ingredient preferences of a "New England Boiled Dinner" are as diverse as the cooks who make them! Start with this recipe and then make changes as desired. The next day, serve Red Flannel Hash (below) for another favorite Down East meal.

1 (4-5 lb.) BRISKET or CORNED BEEF
COLD WATER
3 Tbsp. SUGAR
4 cloves GARLIC, chopped
1 tsp. PICKLING SPICE
2 BAY LEAVES
2 TURNIPS, chunked
10-12 BEETS, peeled and chunked

6 lg. CARROTS,
    peeled, chunked
4 ONIONS, chunked
6 POTATOES, peeled
    and chunked
1 lg. CABBAGE,
    quartered

Rinse corned beef and place in a large kettle; cover with cold water. Add sugar, garlic, pickling spice and bay leaves. Bring to a boil and boil for 5 minutes. Skim surface, reduce heat, cover and simmer for 2 1/2-3 hours or until meat is tender. In a separate pot, boil beets for 45 minutes or until tender. Add turnips, carrots and onions to meat kettle, adding water as necessary to keep vegetables covered; cook for 1/2 hour. Add potatoes; simmer for 1/2 hour then add cabbage wedges and beets and simmer 15 minutes more. Remove bay leaves and arrange all on a large platter. Serve with **HORSERADISH**, **MUSTARD** and **VINEGAR** on the side.

Red Flannel Hash

Leftover YANKEE BOILED DINNER BEEF and VEGETABLES
3-4 strips BACON
SALT and PEPPER

In a bowl, combine corned beef and vegetables thoroughly and mash well. In a large skillet, fry bacon until crisp; remove, drain and then crumble. Add bacon to meat mixture and season as desired. Add meat mixture to skillet and fry until crusty on the bottom and heated through.

Potato Sticks with Glazed Pork & Cabbage

Maine Potato Board—Presque Isle

1 med. ONION, thinly sliced
1 tsp. BUTTER
3 cups shredded CABBAGE
1 lb. POTATOES, cut into 1/4-inch x 2 1/2-inch sticks
1 lb. boneless PORK TENDERLOIN or CHOPS, fat removed,
   cut into 1/2-inch x 1-inch x 2 1/2 inch strips
1/2 tsp. PAPRIKA
1/2 cup BARBECUE SAUCE
1 Tbsp. DIJON-TYPE MUSTARD

In a 12-inch, round microwaveable platter, place onion and butter. Microwave, uncovered, on High for 1-2 minutes or until onion has slightly softened. Add cabbage. Toss well to mix. Cover tightly with plastic wrap, turning back one edge to vent steam. Microwave on High for 2-3 minutes. Push cabbage mixture to center of platter. Arrange potatoes in a ring around the outer 2 inches of platter. Place pork strips between cabbage and potatoes. Sprinkle with paprika. Microwave, covered, on High for 10-12 minutes or until pork is cooked through and potatoes are tender. In a bowl, mix together barbecue sauce and mustard. Spoon half over the pork. Microwave on High for 2-3 minutes to glaze meat. Serve with remaining sauce.

Serves 4-6.

About Potatoes

Some say that potatoes are fattening—to be accurate, the potato is really 80% water. It's the toppings we put on it which add to the calories and fat.

A Pound of Potatoes is . . .
- about 3 medium potatoes
- 3 cups peeled and sliced
- 2 1/4 cups peeled and diced
- 2 cups mashed
- 2 cups French fries

Breads & Muffins

Mildred's Pumpkin Bread

"This bread freezes well."

Mildred Clements—Lewiston

4 EGGS	3 cups WHOLE-WHEAT FLOUR
1/2 cup WATER	2 tsp. BAKING SODA
1 cup OIL	1 tsp. CINNAMON
1 cup packed BROWN SUGAR	1 tsp. NUTMEG
1 1/4 cups MOLASSES	1/2 tsp. CLOVES
1 cup cooked, mashed PUMPKIN	1 tsp. SALT

Preheat oven to 350°. Grease and flour 2 loaf pans. In a large bowl, beat eggs until fluffy. Beat in water and oil. Mix in sugar and molasses. Add pumpkin. Blend well. Mix in flour, baking soda, cinnamon, nutmeg, cloves and salt. Beat until smooth. Pour batter into loaf pans. Bake for 45-55 minutes or until loaves test done. Let loaves cool in pan for 15 minutes. Turn out on a wire rack.

Anadama Bread

"This bread dough needs no kneading or shaping."

Elizabeth Dooley—Biddeford

3/4 cup BOILING WATER
1/4 cup MOLASSES
1/2 cup + 1 Tbsp. CORNMEAL
3 Tbsp. SHORTENING
SALT
1/4 cup WARM WATER

1 pkg. (.25 oz.) ACTIVE
 DRY YEAST
1 EGG
2 3/4 cups FLOUR
melted BUTTER

In a bowl, combine boiling water, molasses, 1/2 cup cornmeal, shortening and salt. Cool to lukewarm. In another bowl, add warm water and stir in yeast. Add yeast to molasses mixture. Add egg and half of flour. Using an electric mixer, beat for 2 minutes on medium-high speed. (If mixing by hand, use about 325 strokes.) Scrape batter from sides frequently. Add remaining flour. Mix until well-blended. Spread dough evenly in a greased 8 x 4 glass loaf pan. Sprinkle a tablespoon of cornmeal and a little salt over the top; cover. Set in a warm place for about 1 1/2 hours until dough doubles in size. Bake in a 300° oven for 45 minutes. Remove bread from pan immediately and cool on rack. Brush top with melted butter.

Biddeford

Biddeford and its sister city, Saco, are the cultural and commercial centers of this area. The Saco branch of the University of South Maine and the University of New England are located here. The La Kermesse Festival in June celebrates the area's French-Canadian heritage. The St. Mary's Festival in July honors the Irish background of many of Biddeford's residents. The East Point Sanctuary at nearby Biddeford Pool consists of 30 acres of rocky coastal headland and is considered to be one of the best bird watching sites in southern Maine.

Pumpkin Bread

"This is also a great pumpkin muffin recipe, but note that it takes a little longer for the bread to bake than the muffins."

Linda Leigh—Washington

2/3 cup SHORTENING
2 2/3 cups SUGAR
4 EGGS
1 cup PUMPKIN
2/3 cup WATER
3 1/3 cups FLOUR

2 tsp. BAKING SODA
1/2 tsp. BAKING POWDER
1 tsp. CINNAMON
1 tsp. CLOVES
2/3 cup chopped NUTS
2/3 cup RAISINS

In a bowl, cream shortening and sugar together. Stir in eggs, one at a time. Blend. Add pumpkin and water. Mix well. Add flour, baking soda and baking powder. Mix well. Add cinnamon, cloves, nuts and raisins. Mix well. Pour batter into 2 greased loaf pans. Bake in a 350° oven for 45-50 minutes or until loaves test done.

Note: If making muffins, grease a 12-cup muffin tin. Pour batter into cups. Bake in a 350° oven for 7-10 minutes or until muffins test done.

Cheddar Cheese Bread

3 EGGS
3/4 cup WARM MILK
1 Tbsp. HONEY
1/4 cup OIL
2 1/2 cups FLOUR
1 pkg. (.25 oz.) ACTIVE DRY YEAST

1/2 tsp. SALT
2 cups grated CHEDDAR
   CHEESE
1/4 cup toasted SESAME
   SEEDS

In a bowl, combine and beat together eggs and milk. Stir in honey and oil. In another bowl, combine half of the flour with yeast, salt, cheese and half of the sesame seeds. Add to the egg mixture and beat until well-blended. Add the remaining flour. Form dough into a ball, place in a greased bowl and let rise in a warm place for 1 hour. Preheat oven to 350°. Grease a 9 x 5 loaf pan. Arrange dough in pan. Sprinkle remaining sesame seeds on top and bake for 45 minutes.

Passamaquoddy Molasses Cake

This bread is a staple food of the Passamaquoddy Indians.

Waponahki Museum—Perry

1 cup SUGAR
1 cup MOLASSES
1 cup HOT TEA
1 tsp. BAKING SODA
1/4 cup OIL or melted
    SHORTENING

1/2 tsp. GINGER
3/4 cup CINNAMON
Pinch of ALLSPICE
FLOUR
RAISINS

In a bowl, combine sugar and molasses together. Add hot tea and blend well. Stir in baking soda, oil and spices. Add enough flour to batter until mixture resembles cake or pancake batter. Fold in raisins. Pour into a greased and floured 13 x 9 pan and bake in a 375° oven for 30-35 minutes.

Passamaquoddy Indians

Passmaquoddy means "people who fish for pollock." Archaeological evidence indicates these Native Americans have inhabited this land and waterways for at least 3,000 years. The Waponahki Museum is located at the Pleasant Point Passamaquoddy Reservation next to Perry near the eastern tip of Maine.

Tom Francis

This is a recipe of the Passamaquoddy people. It is similar to the dough for Navajo Indian Fry Bread.

Waponahki Museum—Perry

2 cups FLOUR
2 tsp. BAKING POWDER
1/2 tsp. SALT

1/2 tsp. SUGAR
SPRING WATER or MILK

In a bowl, combine all dry ingredients. Add just enough liquid to make batter desired consistency. Ladle mixture into skillet and fry in oil on medium-high heat until brown. Drain on paper towels and serve.

These three recipes are from the Country Classics *cookbook by the volunteer fire department of Montville.*

Colonial Brown Bread

4 cups WHOLE-WHEAT FLOUR
1 1/3 cups WHITE FLOUR
2 cups packed BROWN SUGAR
4 tsp. BAKING SODA
1 tsp. SALT
4 cups BUTTERMILK

Add flours to a mixing bowl. Stir in brown sugar, baking soda and salt. Stir and slowly add buttermilk continuing to stir until all is blended. Pour into 2 large loaf pans. Bake at 350° for 1 hour.

Gingerbread

1 cup DARK MOLASSES
1/2 cup OIL
1/2 tsp. CLOVES
1 tsp. GINGER
1/2 tsp. NUTMEG
1/2 cup BROWN SUGAR
2 1/2 cups FLOUR
1 tsp. BAKING SODA
1 cup BOILING WATER

In a bowl, blend together the first seven ingredients. In another bowl, dissolve baking soda in boiling water, then blend into molasses mixture. Pour batter into a greased 8 x 8 baking pan and bake at 350° for 30 minutes.

Oatmeal Bread

1 cup ROLLED OATS
2 cups BOILING WATER
2 Tbsp. BUTTER
2 tsp. SALT
1/2 cup MOLASSES
1 env. (.25 oz.) YEAST
1/2 cup WARM WATER
5-6 cups FLOUR

Place oats in a bowl and combine with boiling water; stir in butter, salt and molasses. In another bowl, dissolve yeast in warm water. Combine both mixtures, then stir in enough flour so that dough is no longer sticky. Place dough on a floured board and knead until smooth then place in a greased bowl and set in a warm area to let double in bulk, about 1 hour. Shape dough into 2 loaves, place in loaf pans and let rise again until doubled in size. Bake at 350° for 50-60 minutes or until lightly browned and tests done.

Hot Onion Bread

"An easy, delicious and impressive bread to make for guests."

Eunice Scarborough—Auburn

2 med. ONIONS
3 Tbsp. MARGARINE
2 cups FLOUR, sifted
3 tsp. BAKING POWDER
1 tsp. SALT

2/3 cup MILK
1 EGG
1 cup SOUR CREAM
1 tsp. POPPY SEEDS

Peel and thinly slice onions into rings. In a skillet, melt margarine and gently sauté onions for 10-15 minutes. Do not brown. In a bowl, combine flour, baking powder and 1/2 teaspoon salt. Add milk and mix well. Grease an 8 x 8 baking pan. Spread dough on the bottom of the pan. Top with the onions. In a bowl, beat egg with sour cream and remaining salt. Pour over onions. Sprinkle poppy seeds on top. Bake in a 375° oven for 30 minutes or until topping is set. Serve hot.

Pear Bread

"In the autumn, when pears are in the market, I usually make this bread and freeze some to enjoy all winter."

Eunice Scarborough—Auburn

1 cup LEMON YOGURT
2 EGGS
1/3 cup MILK
1/4 cup OIL
2 cups FLOUR
1/2 cup packed BROWN SUGAR

1/2 cup WHEAT GERM
1 Tbsp. BAKING POWDER
1/4 tsp. ground CORIANDER
1 tsp. SALT
1 1/2 cups chopped PEARS

Preheat oven to 350°. In a bowl, combine yogurt and eggs. Beat together. Add milk and oil; blend. Add flour, brown sugar, wheat germ, baking powder, coriander and salt. Beat well. Gently fold in pears. Grease a 9 x 5 loaf pan. Pour batter into loaf pan and bake for 60-70 minutes. Test for doneness. If top browns before bread is done, cover loosely with a piece of foil.

Maine Blueberries

Blueberries that once grew wild in Maine are now culti-vated and have become a major product. Maine grows 98% of the wild blueberry crop in the United States.

Storing Blueberries

Fresh wild blueberries are perishable and should be refrig-erated until they are ready to be used. Once chilled, they will last at peak flavor for two weeks. Do not wash berries before freezing. The secret to successfully freezing wild berries is to freeze them when they are completely dry. Remember, once defrosted, they cannot be refrozen. When freezing a large quantity of blueberries, place them in layers on a cookie sheet and put them directly into the freezer. As soon as they are frozen (they should be hard and roll like marbles) they can be packed into plastic bags or containers. Frozen berries will store well for up to two years. When used for baking, frozen blueberries do not have to be defrosted (pancakes included).

Blueberry Gingerbread

Angela Marsh—Augusta

1/2 cup SHORTENING	1/2 tsp. SALT
1 cup + 3 Tbsp. SUGAR	1 tsp. BAKING SODA
1 EGG	1 cup SOUR MILK or
2 cups sifted FLOUR	BUTTERMILK
1 tsp. CINNAMON	3 Tbsp. MOLASSES
1/2 tsp. GINGER	1 cup BLUEBERRIES

Cream shortening and 1 cup of sugar, add egg and beat. Sift together flour, cinnamon, ginger, salt and baking soda. Stir into creamed mixture. Blend in milk and molasses. Fold in blueber-ries. Pour into an 8 x 8 baking pan that has been greased on the bottom only. Sprinkle top with remaining sugar. Bake in a 350° oven for 50-60 minutes or until bread tests done.

Wild Blueberry Nut Bread

Wild Blueberry Commission of Maine—Orono

3 cups WHITE FLOUR
1 Tbsp. BAKING POWDER
1/4 tsp. BAKING SODA
1 cup SUGAR
1 cup chopped PECANS

3 lg. EGGS
1 cup MILK
1/2 cup melted BUTTER, cooled
1 1/2 cups WILD BLUEBERRIES

Preheat oven to 350°. In a large bowl, combine flour, baking powder, baking soda, sugar and pecans. Stir thoroughly. In another bowl, beat eggs, milk and butter until well-blended. Pour egg mixture over dry ingredients. Stir until completely moistened. Do not beat. Gently fold in blueberries. Pour batter into a well-greased 9 x 5 loaf pan. Set aside for 10 minutes. Bake for 1 hour or until loaf tests done. Cool bread upright in pan for 20 minutes, then turn out onto rack. Cool completely before cutting.

Yummy Blueberry Cake

Alice Alpie—Washington

2 EGGS, separated
1 cup SUGAR
1/2 cup MARGARINE
1 1/2 cups FLOUR
1 tsp. BAKING POWDER

1/3 cup MILK
1 tsp. VANILLA
1 1/2 cups BLUEBERRIES
SUGAR, as desired
WHIPPED CREAM

In a bowl, beat egg whites until soft peaks form. Gradually add 1/4 cup of sugar. Beat until stiff; set aside. In another bowl, cream margarine and 3/4 cup of sugar together. Beat in the egg yolks. In another bowl, combine flour and baking powder; add alternately to the creamed mixture with milk. Blend well. Stir in vanilla. Fold in egg whites. Toss berries with one tablespoon of flour; fold into batter. Place mixture in an 8-inch square baking pan. Sprinkle top with sugar. Bake in a 350° oven for 40-45 minutes. Remove to a wire rack and cool. When ready to serve, top with whipped cream.

Wild Blueberry Pan Dowdy

"This is our birthday cake. No other will do."

Charlene Shephard—Hancock

2 cups WILD BLUEBERRIES
1/3 cup SUGAR
JUICE of 1/2 LEMON
1/2 cup BUTTER
1/2 cup SUGAR
1 EGG

1 1/2 cups sifted FLOUR
2 tsp. BAKING POWDER
1/2 tsp. SALT
1/2 cup MILK
CREAM

Preheat oven to to 375°. In a saucepan, combine berries with 1/3 cup sugar and lemon juice. Cook, uncovered, stirring constantly for 5 minutes. Pour into a well-greased 9 x 9 baking pan. Set aside. In a mixing bowl, cream butter until light. Gradually beat in 1/2 cup sugar and stir in egg. Sift flour, baking powder and salt together. Add alternately with milk to butter/sugar mixture. With each addition, beat until smooth. Spread over berries. Bake for 20 minutes. Add cream to top of each serving.

Blueberry Gems

"If it is out of season for fresh blueberries, frozen berries can be substituted in this recipe."

Steve Ludden—Wells

1 1/2 cups FLOUR
1/4 cup SUGAR
1 1/2 tsp. BAKING POWDER
1/4 tsp. SALT
2 EGG WHITES

2/3 cup ORANGE JUICE
2 Tbsp. OIL
1 tsp. VANILLA
1 cup BLUEBERRIES

In a bowl, combine flour, sugar, baking powder and salt. In another bowl, combine and beat egg whites, orange juice, oil and vanilla; fold into dry ingredients, stirring just until moistened. Fold in blueberries. Spray 3/4-inch muffin cup pans with nonstick spray. Fill muffin cups full. Bake in a 400° oven about 17 minutes or until golden. Cool slightly before serving.

Makes 36 muffins.

Wild Blueberry Ravioli

"Here at Frogwater Cafe we serve these raviolis with our homemade caramel sauce or a vanilla bean sauce."

Erin Carey & Joseph Zdanowicz—Frogwater Cafe, Camden

Dough:
   6 oz. BUTTER
   1 1/2 cups FLOUR
   1/4 cup SUGAR
   3 Tbsp. WATER

Filling:
   Fresh BLUEBERRIES
   1 Tbsp. SUGAR

In a mixing bowl, cut butter into flour and sugar until crumbly. Add water to form a shaggy dough; cover and refrigerate at least 30 minutes. Combine blueberries and sugar and stir until berries are well-coated. Divide dough in half and then roll each half out to a very thin rectangle. Mark out one of the rectangles like ravioli squares. Fill center of each square with blueberry mixture, leaving enough room to seal seams. Carefully top with second layer of rolled-out dough. Press down around all ravioli squares to push out air. Using a knife, divide squares. Bake in a 350° oven for 8-12 minutes. Serve with desired sauce.

Blueberry Pie

Theda Lyden—Harraseeket Inn, Freeport

8 cups fresh MAINE BLUEBERRIES   1 tsp. CINNAMON
5 Tbsp. TAPIOCA   1/2 tsp. SALT
1/2 cup BROWN SUGAR   2 (10-inch) PIE CRUSTS
1/2 cup WHITE SUGAR

In a bowl, combine all ingredients except pie crusts. Ladle blueberry mixture into bottom crust. Cover with top crust and prick with a fork to vent. Bake in a 350° oven until center bubbles.

Blueberry Bread

"This is the best!"

Judith Burke—The Keeper's House, Isle au Haut

2 cups FLOUR	2 EGGS, beaten
1 cup SUGAR	1 cup MILK
3 tsp. BAKING POWDER	1 1/2 cups fresh or frozen
1/4 tsp. SALT	BLUEBERRIES
1/2 cup SHORTENING	

In a mixing bowl, sift together 1 3/4 cups flour, sugar, baking powder and salt. Cut in shortening. In another bowl, combine eggs with milk. Gently mix wet ingredients with dry ingredients. In a separate bowl, add blueberries to remaining flour and stir to coat. Fold berries into batter. Pour batter in a greased loaf pan and bake in a 350° oven for 1 hour.

Maine, the Healthful State

Maine is recognized as one of the most healthful states in the nation with summer temperatures averaging 70°F and winter temperatures averaging 20°F.

Blueberry-Oatmeal Pudding

Wild Blueberry Association of North America—Bar Harbor

4 cups fresh BLUEBERRIES	1/3 cup packed BROWN
1/3 cup SUGAR	SUGAR
2 Tsp. LEMON JUICE	1/3 cup FLOUR
4 Tbsp. BUTTER	3/4 cup QUICK-COOKING OATS

Place blueberries in a 1 1/2-quart baking dish. Sprinkle with sugar and lemon juice. Cream butter with brown sugar then blend in flour and oats with a fork. Spread butter mixture over blueberries. Bake in a 375° oven for 35-40 minutes.

Joan's Blueberry Cornmeal Muffins

"Cornmeal fans will love the flavor of these muffins, they are wonderful when served with honey butter. If you gently fold in all of the ingredients, these muffins will be light and fluffy."

Joan Schlosstein—Breakfast Chef at Pilgrim's Inn, Deer Isle

2 1/4 cups FLOUR
1 cup + 2 Tbsp. CORNMEAL
3/4 cup SUGAR
4 1/2 tsp. BAKING POWDER
3 EGGS

5 Tbsp. UNSALTED BUTTER, melted
1 1/2 cups BUTTERMILK
1 cup BLUEBERRIES

Preheat oven to 375°. Grease 24 (2 1/2-inch) muffin cups or line with paper baking cups. In a bowl, combine flour, cornmeal, sugar and baking powder. In another bowl, whisk together eggs, butter and buttermilk. Gently stir into dry ingredients, just until combined. Fold in blueberries. Fill prepared muffin tins 3/4 full. Bake for 25-30 minutes or until toothpick inserted in center comes out clean. Cool on a wire rack.

Wild Blueberry Pie

Wild Blueberry Association of North America—Bar Harbor

2 (9-inch) PIE CRUSTS
1 Tbsp. WHITE FLOUR
2 Tbsp. CORNSTARCH
1/2 cup SUGAR

1/8 tsp. CINNAMON
1/8 tsp. SALT
5 cups WILD BLUEBERRIES
1/2 tsp. grated LEMON PEEL

Preheat oven to 425°. Line pie pan with one of the crusts. In a bowl, combine flour, cornstarch, sugar, cinnamon and salt. Mix well. Add wild blueberries and lemon peel. Stir. Pour mixture into pie crust. Slice remaining crust into strips and create a lattice top for the pie. Crimp edges. Bake for 10 minutes, then lower heat to 350°. Bake for 30-40 minutes or until top is browned. Cool before slicing.

Blueberries & Dumplings

*"My mother used to make these for our family and
we all loved them."*

Georgianna Duff—Portland

2 cups firm BLUEBERRIES   **1 cup WATER**
1/2 cup SUGAR   **WHIPPED CREAM**

In a saucepan, combine berries, sugar and water. Bring to a boil over high heat and boil for 1 minute. Add ***Dumpling*** batter to saucepan by tablespoons, spacing about 1 inch apart. Cover pan tightly. Reduce heat to low and simmer for 20 minutes without opening, then test for doneness with a toothpick. Divide dumplings between serving bowls; cover with blueberry mixture and add a dollop of whipped cream to each.

Dumplings

1 cup FLOUR   **1/4 tsp. SALT**
2 tsp. BAKING POWDER   **1/2 cup HALF AND HALF**

In a mixing bowl, combine flour, baking powder and salt until well-blended. Pour in half and half and whip with a spoon until smooth.

Wild Blueberry Jam

*"When blueberries are in season, make this jam
to use throughout the year."*

Georgianna Duff—Portland

3 lbs. WILD BLUEBERRIES   **4 1/2 cups SUGAR**

Sterilize 5 (1/2-pint) jelly glasses and lids. Wash and sort berries, then crush them. In a large saucepan, combine blueberries with sugar. Mix well. Bring to a boil and cook for 15-20 minutes, stirring constantly. Test for doneness. Pour into hot glasses; add lids and process in boiling water bath for 5 minutes.

Maine Blueberry Pancakes

James & Linda Marple—Beaver Hill Farms, Liberty

2 cups FLOUR
2 tsp. BAKING POWDER
1/2 tsp. BAKING SODA
3 Tbsp. SUGAR
1/2 tsp. SALT
1 EGG
1 1/2 cups BUTTERMILK
3 Tbsp. SHORTENING
1 1/2 cups BLUEBERRIES
BUTTER
BEAVER HILL FARMS® MAPLE SYRUP

In a large bowl, sift dry ingredients together. In another bowl, beat egg, stir in buttermilk and shortening. Combine both ingredients. Ladle batter for desired size pancakes onto a hot griddle. Turn to brown both sides. When serving, top with pats of butter and pour syrup generously over all.

Maine Blueberry Buckle

"This is especially good with freshly ripened berries!"

Dorothy Sainio—Washington

2 cups FLOUR
2 tsp. BAKING POWDER
1/2 tsp. SALT
3/4 cup SUGAR

1/4 cup BUTTER or MARGARINE
3/4 cup MILK
1 EGG
1 cup BLUEBERRIES

Topping:
   1/2 cup SUGAR
   1/4 cup FLOUR

   1/2 tsp. CINNAMON
   1/4 cup BUTTER

In a mixing bowl, combine flour, baking powder and salt together. Add sugar and cut in butter. Stir in milk and egg and then fold in blueberries. Pour batter into a greased and floured cake pan. In a small bowl, combine sugar, flour and cinnamon and cream with the butter. Spread topping over berries. Bake in a 375° oven for 40-45 minutes.

Desserts

Cranberry-Poppy Seed Pound Cake

A new crop that Maine is developing is cranberries. It is a large project that the University of Maine is nurturing.

University of Maine—Augusta

2 sticks UNSALTED BUTTER, softened	1/2 tsp. BAKING SODA SALT
2 cups SUGAR	1 Tbsp. GINGER
4 lg. EGGS, room temperature	1/3 cup EVAPORATED MILK
2 1/2 cups FLOUR	2 1/2 cups CRANBERRIES
1 tsp. BAKING POWDER	1/2 cup POPPY SEEDS

In a bowl, cream butter, then add sugar a little at a time while beating with electric mixer. Beat until fluffy. Add eggs, one at a time, beating well after each addition. In another bowl, sift together flour, baking powder, baking soda, salt and ginger. Stir butter mixture and milk alternately into flour mixture. Fold in cranberries and poppy seeds. Spoon into a well-buttered and floured bundt pan. Bake in a 350° oven for 1 1/4 hours or until tests done. Cool for 10 minutes, then turn out onto rack.

Carrot & Raisin Cake
with
Irish Cream Frosting

"This is a recipe that will certainly fit a special occasion."

Annette Guttormsen—Calais

2 1/2 cups FLOUR
1 1/2 Tbsp. DOUBLE-ACTING BAKING POWDER
1/2 tsp. SALT
2 tsp. CINNAMON
1/8 tsp. freshly grated NUTMEG
1/2 tsp. ALLSPICE
1 cup UNSALTED BUTTER, softened
1 cup packed BROWN SUGAR
5 lg. EGGS, separated
1 whole EGG
2 1/2 cups finely grated CARROTS
1/2 cup RAISINS
2 tsp. freshly grated ORANGE PEEL
1/4 cup fresh ORANGE JUICE
POWDERED SUGAR

In a bowl, combine flour, baking powder, salt, cinnamon, nutmeg and allspice. In another bowl, using electric beater, beat butter and brown sugar until mixture is light and fluffy. Beat in egg yolks and one whole egg, one at a time, beating until smooth after each addition. Add carrots, raisins and orange peel. Blend well. Stir in flour mixture alternately with orange juice in 2 batches. Stir batter until blended. Beat egg whites until stiff; fold into batter. Divide batter between 3 buttered and floured 8-inch round cake pans. Spread evenly. Bake in a 350° oven for 30-35 minutes. Let layers cool in pans for 20 minutes. Invert onto racks and let cool completely. (Layers may be made one day ahead. Keep well-wrapped at room temperature.) Invert 1 cake layer onto a plate. Spread 1/3 of the **Irish Cream Frosting** on top. Add second layer. Frost top.

(continued on next page)

Carrot & Raisin Cake with Irish Cream Frosting
(continued from previous page)

Add third layer. Spread frosting on the sides of cake. Place a paper doily on top of cake and sift powdered sugar over it. Remove doily carefully. Put remaining frosting in a pastry bag with a star tip. Pipe *Irish Cream Frosting* decoratively around edges of cake.

Irish Cream Frosting

1 cup UNSALTED BUTTER
2 1/4 cups POWDERED SUGAR
1/2 tsp. SALT
1/4 cup IRISH CREAM LIQUEUR or HEAVY CREAM

In a bowl, cream butter until smooth with an electric mixer. Beat in powdered sugar gradually. Beat in salt and Irish cream. Beat frosting until light and fluffy.

Cheesy Apple Fritters

"This is my Mother's recipe."

Betty Orton—Presque Isle

1 1/2 cups FLOUR
2 tsp. BAKING POWDER
1/2 cup SUGAR
1/4 tsp. CINNAMON
1/2 tsp. SALT
2 EGGS
1/2 cup MILK
2 cups peeled, chopped APPLES
2 cups shredded SHARP CHEDDAR CHEESE
OIL for frying
POWDERED SUGAR

In a bowl, combine flour, baking powder, sugar, cinnamon and salt. In another bowl, beat eggs; stir in milk. Blend into dry ingredients. Fold in apples and cheese. Heat oil to 400°. Carefully drop in spoonfuls of dough. Cook for 3-4 minutes, turning to brown all sides. Drain on paper towels. Roll in powdered sugar.

Gingersnap Cookies

"This was my Great-Grandmother Gagnon's recipe."

Sharon Baldyga—Wells

3/4 cup SHORTENING
1 1/4 cups SUGAR
2 EGGS
1/4 cup MOLASSES
2 cups FLOUR

1 Tbsp. GINGER
2 tsp. BAKING SODA
1 tsp. CINNAMON
1/2 tsp. SALT

In a bowl, cream shortening and 1 cup sugar together. Add eggs and molasses. Mix well. Add dry ingredients and mix well. Chill. Using 1 teaspoon of dough for each cookie, form into balls and roll in remaining sugar. Place on a cookie sheet and bake at 350° for no more than 8 minutes for soft cookies.

Baxter State Park

This wilderness area of over 200,000 acres was a gift to the State of Maine by former governor Percival P. Baxter. In 1933, the area was officially designated as Baxter State Park and the 5,267 ft. summit of Mount Katahdin was named Baxter Peak in his honor.

Indian Pudding

"This is a favorite dessert at our diner."

From the *Maine Courses* Cookbook—The Maine Diner, Wells

1 1/2 qts. MILK
1 1/4 cups MOLASSES
1 1/4 cups CORNMEAL
1 cup SUGAR
1/2 tsp. GINGER

1/2 tsp. CINNAMON
1/2 tsp. NUTMEG
3/4 tsp. SALT
3 EGGS, well-beaten
1 tsp. VANILLA

In a saucepan, heat milk. Add molasses. Cook slowly while stirring constantly. Add all dry ingredients. Continue to stir. Cook until pudding starts to thicken. Add beaten eggs. Remove from heat when it starts to bubble. Stir in vanilla. Let cool.

Dreamy Chocolate Rice Pudding

"We like to serve this version of rice pudding when we want something very special."

Beverly Eaton—Portland

1 1/2 CHOCOLATE SQUARES,
   cut very fine
4 Tbsp. uncooked RICE
1/2 tsp. SALT
3 cups MILK
1/2 cup SUGAR

1/2 cup COLD MILK
2 1/2 tsp. GELATIN
1/3 cup chopped NUTS
1/2 tsp. VANILLA
1/2 cup HEAVY CREAM,
   whipped

In a double boiler, combine chocolate, rice, salt, milk and sugar. Cook for 15 minutes, stirring occasionally. Cover. Cook for 1 1/2 hours more. In a cup, combine cold milk and gelatin. Let stand for 5 minutes. Stir into chocolate and rice mixture. Remove from heat. Chill. When pudding is thick, add nuts and vanilla. Fold in whipped cream.

Strawberry Pie

Frances Schroyer—Washington

2 cups WATER
1 cup SUGAR
1/4 cup + 1 tsp. CORNSTARCH
1 pkg. (3 oz.) STRAWBERRY-BANANA GELATIN
1 qt. fresh STRAWBERRIES
1 (9-inch) baked PIE SHELL
WHIPPED CREAM

In a saucepan, bring water to a boil. Remove from heat. Add sugar and cornstarch. Mix well. Return to stove and bring to a boil. Let cook for a few minutes. Remove from heat. Add gelatin and mix well. Cool. Place rinsed and hulled strawberries in pie shell. Pour cooled mixture evenly over berries. Chill until set. When ready to serve, top with whipped cream.

Strawberry Rhubarb Shortcake

Co-chefs Alex and Aki are a young husband and wife team who create fabulous dishes for guests of the Bradley Inn.

Alex Talbot & Aki Kamozawa—The Bradley Inn, New Harbor

Biscuit:

2 cups FLOUR	1 Tbsp. BAKING POWDER
3 Tbsp. SUGAR	1/2 cup BUTTER
1/2 tsp. SALT	1 cup CREAM

In a food processor, combine dry ingredients and blend. Add butter and pulse briefly. Add cream and pulse just until dough comes together. Roll out dough and cut into 3-inch circles that are 1/2-inch thick. Bake at 375° for 8-10 minutes.

Rhubarb:

3-4 stalks RHUBARB	1/2 cup BROWN SUGAR
2 Tbsp. LIME JUICE	Pinch of SALT

Slice rhubarb diagonally, approximately 1/4-inch thick. Toss with lime juice, sugar and salt. Marinate for several hours.

Strawberries:

1 pint STRAWBERRIES	1 Tbsp. BROWN SUGAR
Squeeze of LIME JUICE	Pinch SALT

Clean and slice strawberries in half. Toss with lime juice, brown sugar and salt. Marinate briefly.

To Serve:

Place 2 tablespoons rhubarb in the center of each serving plate, circle with strawberries and top with **WHIPPED CREAM**. Shake **POWDERED SUGAR** over biscuit and place on top.

Orono

Orono is the home of the University of Maine and the cultural center for the Penobscot Valley. The University was established in 1868 with only two teachers and 12 students. It has become a major research and educational facility.

Mascarpone Cheesecake

The Bradley Inn is a charming old refuge, positioned almost at the tip of the Pemaquid Peninsula, just south of two perfectly beautiful working harbors.

Alex Talbot & Aki Kamozawa—The Bradley Inn, New Harbor

Crust:

1 cup GRAHAM CRACKER CRUMBS

1/4 cup SUGAR

1/4 cup melted BUTTER

Pinch of SALT

Filling:

1/2 cup SUGAR

1 1/2 cups FROMAGE BLANC

Pinch of SALT

2 EGGS

2 tsp. VANILLA

1 ctn. (17 1/2 oz.) MASCARPONE

2 Tbsp. BUTTER, melted

In a bowl, blend crust ingredients together and line an 8- or 9-inch springform pan with mixture. Combine first five filling ingredients in a blender and blend until smooth. Add chunks of Mascarpone cheese to running blender and continue blending until mixture is smooth. Fold in melted butter; pour mixture into prepared pan and bake at 325° for 45 minutes. Cool and chill at least 4 hours before serving.

Note: Fromage Blanc is a very soft French cream cheese-style cheese made from skimmed cow's milk. Mascarpone is a soft, double or triple cream cheese made in Switzerland and Italy from cow's milk.

Cranberry Pie Dessert

"This is a great dessert when fresh cranberries are in season."

Natalie Crowley—Washington

2 cups CRANBERRIES

1 1/2 cups SUGAR

1/2 cup chopped NUTS

2 EGGS

1 cup FLOUR

1/2 cup melted BUTTER

Spread cranberries in the bottom of a lightly greased 9-inch pie plate. In a bowl, combine 1/2 cup sugar and nuts. Sprinkle over cranberries. In another bowl, beat eggs with 1 cup of sugar. Mix in flour and butter. Pour egg mixture over berries. Bake in a 325° oven for 50-60 minutes.

Whoopie Pies

"This recipe was handed down to me from my grandmother and mother—it used to be a family secret!"

James Boudreau—Waterville

2 3/4 cups ALL-PURPOSE FLOUR	1 1/2 cups SUGAR
1 tsp. BAKING SODA	1/2 cup SHORTENING
1 tsp. BAKING POWDER	1 tsp. VANILLA
1/2 tsp. SALT	2 EGGS
1/2 cup HOT WATER	1/2 cup SOUR MILK*
1/2 cup COCOA POWDER	

In a bowl, sift together 3 times the flour, baking soda, baking powder and salt. In another bowl, combine hot water and cocoa. Set aside to cool, then blend with sifted mixture. In a third bowl, cream together sugar, shortening and vanilla until mixture has a pastelike consistency; blend in eggs and sour milk. Combine with flour mixture. Drop batter by spoonfuls onto a greased cookie sheet and bake at 350° for 10-15 minutes, or until centers spring back when lightly touched. When cookies have cooled, spread half of them with a layer of *Whoopie Pie Filling* and then top with another cookie. Wrap each pie individually in clear plastic wrap to store.

Note: Make sour milk by adding 1 teaspoon of white vinegar to 1/2 cup milk.

Whoopie Pie Filling

3 1/2 Tbsp. ALL-PURPOSE FLOUR	3/4 cup SUGAR
3/4 cup MILK	3/4 cup SHORTENING
Pinch of SALT	1/2 tsp. VANILLA

In a saucepan, over medium heat, combine flour, milk and salt and cook for 10 minutes. Set aside to cool. Put sugar, shortening and vanilla in an electric mixer bowl, cream well. Combine both mixtures thoroughly.

Maine Firsts

Founded in 1866, Togus was the first Veteran's Hospital in the United States. The nation's first sawmill was established near York in 1623.

Index

Index (continued)

Index (continued)

★ ★ ★ ★ *Maine Cook Book* ★ ★ ★ ★

Recipe Contributors

Rachel Allen, Waterville 17, 49

James Boudreau, Waterville 88

Shirley Allerton, Augusta 16, 64

Alice Alpie, Washington 44, 74

Sharon Baldyga, Wells 84

Charlotte Barnes, Bar Harbor 20, 21

Chef Wilfred Beriau (www.lovemaine
lobsters.com), S. Portland 30, 32

Exec. Chef Gerald Bonsey, CEC–York Harbor Inn,
York Harbor 13, 40

Martha Browne, Bar Harbor 10

Judith Burke–The Keeper's House, Isle au Haut
34, 43, 57, 77

Erin Carey & Joseph Zdanowicz, Frogwater Cafe,
Camden 52, 76

Shirley Clarke, Portland 43, 51, 53

Mildred Clements, Lewiston 67

Susan Clough–Spruce Point Inn, Boothbay
Harbor 29, 37

Cornforth House Restaurant, Saco 24

Natalie Crowley, Washington 45, 87

Madelyn Cussak, Lewiston 59, 61

Barbara J. Desso, St. Albans 31

Elizabeth Dooley, Biddeford 68

downeastbooks.com 54

Georgianna Duff, Portland 79

Heidi Duffett, Head Chef–Arundel Wharf
Restaurant, Kennebunkport 38, 41

Beverly Eaton, Portland 85

Chef Terry Foster–Pilgrim's Inn Cookbook, Deer
Isle 8, 35, 55

Sonny & Dottie Gibson–North Camps, Oquossoc
59, 61, 63

Chef Christian Gordon–Federal Jack's Restaurant
& Brew Pub, Kennebunkport 50

Bill Graves–Presque Isle 13, 23

The Great Eastern Mussel Farms, Inc., Tenants
Harbor 19, 58

Annette Guttormsen, Calais 46, 82

Chef Michael Ham–Tugboat Inn, Boothbay
Harbor 33

Marjorie Hancock, Brunswick 47

Rita Hanson, Washington 44

Barbara Hayes-Warren, South Portland 15, 54

Tala Henry, Wells 7

Linda Leigh, Washington 69

Larry LeRoy–Medawisla Wilderness
Camps, Greenville 64

Audrey Little, Washington 18, 24

Steve Ludden, Wells 75

Theda Lyden–Harraseeket Inn,
Freeport 22, 76

Maine Dept. Marine Resources, Augusta 18

The Maine Diner, Wells 14, 31, 84

Maine Lobster Promotion Council,
Bangor 28, 36

Maine Potato Board, Presque Isle 11, 20, 66

Dorothy Marple, Liberty 12

James & Linda Marple–Beaver Hill Farms,
Liberty 80

Angela Marsh, Augusta 73

Kenneth McQuire, Bar Harbor 53, 62

Montville Fire Department 71

Judith Nelson, Rockland 9

Shirley Newman, South Portland 58

Evelyn Novotny, Bangor 63

Betty Orton, Presque Isle 83

Carolann Ouellette–Moose Point Tavern,
Jackman 48, 52, 60, 62

Dorothy Ramshuck, Bangor 56

Dorothy Sainio, Washington 80

Emory Sanderson, Augusta 14

Eunice Scarborough, Auburn 12, 72

Joan Schlosstein–Breakfast Chef at
Pilgrim's Inn, Deer Isle 78

Frances Schroyer, Washington 85

Charlene Shepherd, Hancock 75

Greg Smith–Smith's Farm Inc.,
Presque Isle 16

Andrea Swonburg, Portland 39, 45

Alex Talbot & Aki Kamozawa—Bradley Inn,
New Harbor 86-87

Bernice Tompkins, Augusta 22

University of Maine, Augusta 81

Waponahki Museum, Perry 70

Wild Blueberry Assn. of North America, Bar
Harbor 77-78

Wild Blueberry Commission of
Maine, Orono 74

Fran Wilson, Jefferson 51

Cooking Across America Cookbook Collection™

NEW YORK COOK BOOK

New Yorkers are proud of their state and their heritage and it shows in the variety of fabulous foods presented in these pages. *New York Cheesecake, Buffalo Wings, Matzo Ball Soup, Coney Island Hot Dogs, Pasta Fagioli* and many more! 5 1/2 x 8 1/2 — 96 pages . . . $6.95

FLORIDA COOK BOOK

Great recipes from the Sunshine State! Sample *Mango-Champagne Fritters* or *Baked Cheese Papaya, Ham-Tomato Quiche, Florida Blueberry Streusel Coffee Cake, Sautéed Gulf Coast Grouper, Crab & Cheese Pie* or *Drunken Shrimp*. Special Florida seafood section, tasty side dishes and delightful desserts. Includes fascinating facts and trivia. 5 1/2 x 8 1/2 — 96 pages . . . $6.95

VIRGINIA COOK BOOK

Over 140 recipes from all across this great state! From unbeatable seafood recipes to savory ham dishes, crab specialties, delicious apple recipes, tempting peanut delights and a cornucopia of historical and family favorites. Includes Virginia facts and trivia. 5 1/2 x 8 1/2 — 96 pages . . . $6.95

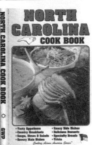

NORTH CAROLINA COOK BOOK

Filled with family favorites as well as recipes that showcase North Carolina's specialty foods. *Sausage Pinwheels, Shipwrecked Crab, Scuppernong Grape Butter, Carolina Blender Slaw, North Carolina Pork BBQ, Rock Fish Muddle, Hushpuppy Fritters, Hummingbird Cake, Peanut Butter Pie*. 5 1/2 x 8 1/2 — 96 pages . . . $6.95

OHIO COOK BOOK

Filled with wonderful and delicious recipes featured in a tantalizing array of mouth-watering family favorites. Try *Apple French Toast, Amish Kidney Bean Salad, Salmon Quiche, Cincinnati "5-Way" Chili, Spinach Tomatofeller, Marble Kuchen, Snickerdoodles, Buckeyes, Cranberry Cake*. 5 1/2 x 8 1/2 — 96 pages . . . $6.95

ORDER BLANK

GOLDEN WEST PUBLISHERS

4113 N. Longview Ave. • Phoenix, AZ 85014

www.goldenwestpublishers.com • **1-800-658-5830** • FAX 602-279-6901

Qty	Title	Price	Amount
	Apple Lovers Cook Book	**6.95**	
	Bean Lovers Cook Book	**6.95**	
	Berry Lovers Cook Book	**6.95**	
	Chili-Lovers' Cook Book	**6.95**	
	Chip and Dip Lovers Cook Book	**6.95**	
	Corn Lovers Cook Book	**6.95**	
	Easy Recipes for Wild Game & Fish	**6.95**	
	Florida Cook Book	**6.95**	
	Illinois Cook Book	**6.95**	
	Indiana Cook Book	**6.95**	
	Joy of Muffins	**6.95**	
	Maine Cook Book	**6.95**	
	New York Cook Book	**6.95**	
	North Carolina Cook Book	**6.95**	
	Ohio Cook Book	**6.95**	
	Pumpkin Lovers Cook Book	**6.95**	
	Salsa Lovers Cook Book	**6.95**	
	Seafood Lovers Cook Book	**6.95**	
	Veggie Lovers Cook Book	**6.95**	
	Virginia Cook Book	**6.95**	
Shipping & Handling Add:	United States $4.00 Canada & Mexico $5.00—All others $12.00		

☐ My Check or Money Order Enclosed

☐ MasterCard ☐ VISA

Total $ _____

(Payable in U.S. funds)

Acct. No. _____ Exp. Date _____

Signature _____

Name _____ Phone _____

Address _____

City/State/Zip _____

Call for a FREE catalog of all of our titles

This order blank may be photo copied.

10/03

ME Ck Bk